THE
BILLION
DOLLAR
WINDFALL

MORTON SHULMAN

THE BILLION DOLLAR WINDFALL

William Morrow and Company, Inc.　New York

To
Beverley Burns
for the idea
and
Alastair Dow
and
Jerry McAuliffe
for the research

The rule is clear. It is unlawful for an insider, such as a majority stockholder, to purchase the stock of minority stockholders without disclosing material facts affecting the value of the stock, known to the majority stockholder by virtue of his inside position but not known to the selling minority stockholders, which information would have affected the judgment of the sellers. The duty of disclosure stems from the necessity of preventing a corporate insider from utilizing his position to take unfair advantage of the uninformed minority stockholders. It is an attempt to provide some degree of equalization of bargaining position in order that the minority may exercise an informed judgment in any such transaction....One of the primary purposes of the Securities Exchange Act of 1934 was to outlaw the use of inside information by corporate officers and principal stockholders for their own financial advantage to the detriment of uninformed public security holders.

Judge Paul Leahy, in his opinion,
Speed v. Transamerica Corp. (1951).

When an insider has possession of facts which are known to him by virtue of his status and which, if known generally, would tend materially to affect the price of the security, the law requires that the insider disclose these facts to those with whom he deals or forgo the transaction.

William L. Cary,
Former Chairman of the SEC,
in the *Harvard Business Review* (1962).

CONTENTS

INTRODUCTION

This is a true story about those human emotions we normally deny in ourselves and assign only to distant others – greed, lust, selfishness, unfaithfulness, dishonesty – it is the story of the discovery of an orebody worth over $2 billion, and how human beings from every walk of life were affected by the discovery. It is a story of real people. No names have been changed.

There are three dates of particular significance in this story; the first is November 8, 1963, when four French-Canadian laborers at a remote campsite in northern Ontario guided a diamond-tipped drill into the rotted vegetation and finely grained clay that was left when the last of the great continental glaciers receded from this part of Canada eight to ten thousand years ago.

Eighteen feet below that surface of swamp and muskeg lay

a body of ore rich in zinc and copper and silver; it may be years before the outline of that orebody is accurately delineated. In any event it is one of the largest and richest base metals mines in the world.

On November 8, shares of Texas Gulf Sulphur Company, the world's largest sulphur producer, were $17 each on the New York Stock Exchange.

The second date is April 12, 1964, when Texas Gulf Sulphur Company, a large and very conservative corporation, issued a statement to the press:

> During the past few days, the exploration activities of Texas Gulf Sulphur in the area of Timmins, Ontario, have been widely reported in the press, coupled with rumors of a substantial copper discovery there. These reports exaggerate the scale of operations, and mention plans of statistics of size and grade of ore that are without factual basis and have evidently originated by speculation of people not connected with TGS. . . .
>
> The work done to date has not been sufficient to reach definite conclusions and any statement as to size and grade of ore would be premature and possibly misleading. When we have progressed to the point where reasonable and logical conclusions can be made, TGS will issue a definite statement to its stockholders and to the public in order to clarify the Timmins project.

The next day, largely as a result of this carefully prepared announcement, the ten million shares of Texas Gulf, although they sold at a new high of $32.00, then traded down to $30.87.

The third date is April 16, 1964. Prodded by speculative news stories in the *New York Times* and the *New York Herald Tribune*, Texas Gulf President Claude Stephens met his 11 directors for their monthly meeting on the 55th-floor board room of Texas Gulf's head office in Manhattan's Pan Am building. Only two of the directors – Stephens, a 55-year-old

Mississippi-born petroleum engineer, and Charles F. Fogarty, executive vice-president, a mining engineer – knew the results of the Timmins exploration program.

The meeting ended about 10 o'clock, when reporters were called in. Another press release was issued:

> Texas Gulf Sulphur Company has made a major discovery of zinc, copper and silver in the Timmins area of Ontario, Canada. . . .
>
> This is a major discovery. Preliminary data indicate a reserve of more than 25 million tons of ore. The only hole assayed so far represents over 600 feet of ore, representing a true ore thickness of nearly 400 feet. . . .

As soon as the press release was read, the reporter for Dow Jones Inc. raced from the room to the nearest telephone. At 10.55 a.m. the first official announcement of the significance of Texas Gulf's discovery was carried across the "broad tape", the teletype network that services brokerage offices and newspapers across the country.

At the close of stock market trading that day, the price of Texas Gulf shares had climbed from $34 to $37. Two weeks later the stock was at $58; a year later it was $70; ultimately, Texas Gulf stock rose to above $130 per share.

One year and three days after that fateful press conference, the Securities and Exchange Commission issued a complaint in the United States Court for the Southern District of New York.

The complaint charged that Texas Gulf Sulphur had issued on April 12 a press release that was false and misleading and that 13 of its officers, directors, and employees had used information not generally available to the public in order to make personal stock market profits. The SEC said that even the first drill hole in November, 1963, "gave substantial indication, if not proof, that Texas Gulf had discovered a mine of immeasurable value."

Texas Gulf replied that "no such conclusion can ever be drawn from any single hole, even if the drill core is solid gold." Texas Gulf further pleaded that the SEC would have been the first to complain if any optimistic conclusions had been drawn after that first drill hole.

What makes the case against Texas Gulf Sulphur Company so fascinating is not so much that it deals with the discovery of a fabulously rich mine, even though man's primeval urge for wealth has always been attracted by this possibility, nor that it gave everyone – even those softened by urbanization – a chance to participate in the profits and risks of finding a mine without suffering the physical hardships. Its significance goes far beyond the 60,000 shareholders of Texas Gulf, or even the 23 million people in the United States who own stock.

The Texas Gulf case involves everyone who is part of the New Industrial State; it has to do with the new responsibilities that have arisen since the people who run giant corporations have become managers and servants of the shareholders, rather than owner-entrepreneurs. It also questions the responsibility of government agencies such as the Securities and Exchange Commission in pursuing what they consider to be their duty to the public.

The discovery of the mine that became known as Kidd Creek is not a narrow phenomenon with a localized stock market aftermath. It aroused the imagination and suspicions and frequently the greed of tens of thousands of people. Ultimately, it resulted in the shareholders of one company making one billion dollars in capital gains; it allowed dozens of hot-shot unethical promoters to make millions of dollars by selling worthless stock; it caused thousands of gullible market gamblers to lose their shirts; it allowed a few lawyers to make small fortunes in litigation; and it caused one previously respected lady mine developer, the "Queen Bee" of the North, to go to jail.

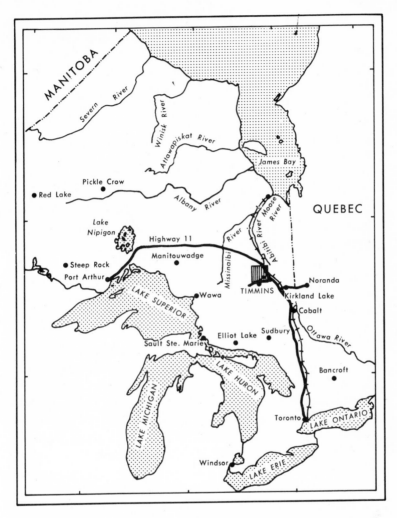

Timmins – the northern Ontario town where the discovery was made.

Chapter One

THE DISCOVERY

The presence of Texas Gulf Sulphur Company in the northern Ontario town of Timmins during that second week of November, 1963, took the form of one 29-year-old geologist who was supposed to be on vacation and six French Canadians hired, without the authority of the company's senior management, to man a drill rig 14 miles northeast of town.

Timmins is a cold town; the temperature there lingers below zero in the winter, and the wind whips across the surrounding flat, featureless terrain. It would be bush wilderness had gold not been discovered there in 1909; with that discovery, the prospectors took over from the railroad builders the role of pioneering the development of Canada's North. In 50 years, more than fifteen hundred million dollars' worth of gold has been extracted from the rock fault that creases by Timmins. The residents of Timmins have a lot of old-fashioned pride in the gold that has been taken from the storied mines of Hollinger, McIntyre and Dome. It was gold that attracted French Canadians and Italians and other first- and second-generation Europeans to the area. But what promised wealth for others yielded only a lifetime of working underground for these people; Timmins has more than its share of beer parlors and chest inspection clinics.

The town is located on the sandy east bank of the Mattagami River, the only spot that survived a ravaging forest fire that killed a hundred persons in 1911. It is 425 road miles north of Toronto and lies beside Highway 11, Ontario's main north-south artery. There is a peculiar spirit in Timmins: dogged and independent and stubborn, never waning.

The town threatened to become another Deadwood Gulch in the early 1930s, but when President Franklin Roosevelt raised the price of gold from $20.67 to $35 an ounce in 1934, old mines re-opened and prospecting flourished once again. The population of Timmins rose in seven years from 11,000 to 30,000. After the war, inflation threatened to close down several of the gold mines, and only Canadian government subsidies kept many of them operating.

Unlike base metals, gold does not float with the economy. Costs rise, ore reserves deplete and become more difficult and expensive to mine, but the price of gold remains constant. By the 1950s, when the mines were closing, Timmins attempted a brave but ineffective campaign to turn its surrounding forlorn muskeg and bush into a tourist area.

Kenneth Darke, an intense young geologist, first came to Timmins in 1959, less than three years after graduating from the University of British Columbia. Darke had joined Texas Gulf for two main reasons: He was promised the chance to travel extensively, and also the opportunity to examine and work on projects of diversified mineralogy and geology. It was a promise that Texas Gulf kept; from the time he first visited Timmins until he returned almost in secrecy four years later, Darke worked in a dozen widely separated parts of the North American continent, never spending more than four months in one place.

In October of 1963 he was anxious to get back to Timmins. For one thing, Timmins bore certain similarities to his home town of Trail, British Columbia, another mining community. More important, Timmins was on the outer margin of the Canadian Shield and lay in the kind of geological environment that he and a few others in Texas Gulf had become convinced provided some of the best overall exploration target areas available.

In those earlier days, Darke had on two separate occasions examined in detail one of the rock outcrops in the Kidd Township area. A trapper had lived on the outcrop 15 or 20 years earlier, and the rock was subsequently examined by dozens of geologists. After his first visit Darke made a second trip for the express purpose of examining in detail the periphery of the outcrop, where he had found tuffs (concentrations of volcanic dust and ash) and what appeared to be pinheads of mineralization. It might have been pyrite (a brass-yellow mineral composed of iron sulphide, popularly called "fool's gold"), but Darke was convinced it was copper mineralization.

By itself, the evidence he gathered from the rock outcrop meant very little. But directly to the north and east, Texas Gulf aerial surveys had indicated that the ground contained conductive material, the first clue to the presence of a mine. On May 28, 1959, he had written in a memorandum to his immediate superior, "The presence of disseminated chalcopyrite [a sulphide copper ore] in the general mineralized zone enhances the possibilities of this sulphide body containing economic minerals."

In the four intervening years, Texas Gulf had been prevented from further investigations of the area that lay next to the rock outcrop – the land was not open for staking because it belonged to a private estate. In June 1963, Texas Gulf finally acquired an option to purchase mineral rights to the property for $500. Darke was anxious to look at it when he arrived in Timmins on October 16.

He had no illusions about his association with Texas Gulf, the world's biggest and lowest-cost sulphur producer. In its heyday in 1955, the company had earned $32,356,000 or $3.23 for each of its ten million shares. As sulphur prices declined, so did Texas Gulf profits. By 1960 earnings were down to $1.27 per share, and by 1963, they were further depressed to less than $1.

The effect of this drop in earnings was that Texas Gulf, although embarked upon a determined program to diversify into minerals other than sulphur, was less than carefree about the expenditure of funds for basic exploration. In 1962 the company had closed its Toronto exploration office, and that same year Texas Gulf slashed its dividends from the 25¢ per share it had been paying for several years to 10¢. In the annual report, the company referred in a foreboding tone to "large expenditures for exploration" and gave this as one of the reasons that its cash position was "substantially reduced."

Darke was unhappy that this was the only reference in the annual report to the company's metals exploration on its Canadian Shield program. Although Texas Gulf had been committed to an extensive exploration program on the shield – and had spent substantial amounts on the project – Darke knew there was a squeeze. Texas Gulf had never altogether cured its split personality; there were still those in management who saw sulphur as the certain, if fluctuating, source of income; exploration, as such, cost money but promised no revenues.

Texas Gulf, in any event, was not a big spender relative to other companies exploring the shield. International Nickel Company of Canada, with enormous nickel deposits 125 miles southwest of Timmins in the Sudbury basin, was the colossus in the area. Both Inco and Falconbridge Nickel Company dwarfed Texas Gulf in terms of exploration budget, equipment, and personnel.

In fact, although Texas Gulf had been active there for six years, and also had major gas holdings in western Canada, the company was little known outside the mining profession. When Darke and another Texas Gulf geologist had amazingly survived a mountaintop crash on an arctic peak, the two were identified in Canadian magazines and newspapers only as employees of "an American mine development company."

Alone in Timmins on behalf of Texas Gulf was Ken Darke. He had just returned from a summer on the northern tip of Baffin Island, 2,000 miles north, where he was helping to outline large lead-zinc deposits. It was years since he had taken a full vacation; in the preceding two years he had done geological evaluation on the Alaskan Wrangall and Brooks Ranges, the Hualapai Mountains of Arizona, and the Solitario Mountains of Texas; besides that, he had assisted in the discovery and development of new Texas Gulf ventures in soda ash in Wyoming and in phosphate in North Carolina.

Darke, before going to Baffin Island, had met with the company's chief geologist, Walter Holyk, and offered to forego his vacation once again if he could spend a month in Timmins. Holyk, another British Columbian, had been at Texas Gulf since 1952 and was the man who initiated the company's Canadian Shield project in 1957. As Holyk described it to me:

In the spring of 1957, I hired Dr. Leo J. Miller and requested that he undertake a program of regional geological studies, compilations, eliminations and gradual selection of areas considered favorable to the occurrence of orebodies. Miller was instructed to concentrate on geological environments similar to that proven to be important in New Brunswick.

During the summer of 1958, Miller examined an outcrop of rock in the northeast corner of Kidd Township on the basis of a reference in the Ontario Department of Mines report describing sparse sulphide mineralization. This site eventually turned out to be the site of the Kidd Creek orebody. Miller considered this region to be very favorable to the occurrence of a sulphide deposit.

The airborne e-m equipment developed by Texas Gulf Sulphur was put into service in early March, 1959. After testing out the equipment on known sulphide zones, Miller flew to the outcrop he was familiar with and considered favorable in northeast Kidd Township, and found a significant anomaly, immediately to the east of the known outcrop, in the first few minutes of flying.

Once the snow was gone, I instructed Darke to examine the Kidd zone anomaly found by Miller in the area Miller considered to be most favorable for the occurrence of a sulphide deposit. Darke mapped such outcrops as were found and concurred with Miller's favorable opinion of the outcrop area.

What excited Darke and Holyk, and to a lesser extent the management of Texas Gulf, was a quarter-mile patch of muskeg and alder bush 14 miles to the north of Timmins. Texas Gulf called it the Murray Hendrie property after the estate which owned it and which, after four years of careful negotiations, had optioned it to Texas Gulf earlier that year.

On the Hendrie property, Texas Gulf's survey crews had detected an anomaly – a reaction recorded by geophysical instruments in which there is a variation from the norm.

Anomalies may indicate the presence of some conductive or magnetic material below the surface of the ground and are a clue to the possible presence of economic minerals. Anomalies abound in the area around Timmins, and most are worthless. Texas Gulf, in fact, had spent close to $3 million finding and drilling 65 anomalies in the preceding four years with no results.

Holyk met Darke's request to go to Timmins, and offered to put at his disposal sufficient funds to carry on the exploration program. Darke's first move was to hire a plane, a Cessna 180, in order to check out the access roads into the area of the Hendrie property. (Since Texas Gulf had first flown over the property by helicopter in 1959, there had been a substantial growth of bush. At the same time, McIntyre-Porcupine Mines Ltd., one of the world's biggest gold producers, had been cutting birch trees from the property for use as support posts in its mine near Timmins. Consequently, the area around the Hendrie property was barely recognizable on the basis of 1957 aerial photos.)

Darke then rented a jeep and drove north from Timmins via an emergency road used to service hydro power lines. When the mudholes made the road too rough to take the jeep further, Darke set out on foot, finally bearing west from the service road and along a muskeg trail used for hauling pulpwood when the winter freeze-up made it possible. The trip took two and a half hours, most of it on foot.

Darke paced up and down what he thought would be the outlines of the 160-acre plot hoping to find accurate boundaries. Kidd is a "surveyed" township, but some of the lines had been laid out 50 years before, and the wood posts that marked the corners of the property had rotted into the swamp and muskeg. Giving himself time to get back to the jeep before nightfall, he returned to the Bon Air Motel.

Darke's first priority was to find someone in whom he could

have absolute trust, someone to help him cut through the alders, willows, tamarack, and spruce that grew from the gooey swamp. When airborne surveys show the presence of an anomaly, the second explorative step is the collection of further information by ground surveys.

At his motel Darke drew up plans for a grid, a series of lines cut at spaced intervals along which geophysical instruments can be carried. He plotted the grid's baseline along a southerly path which, as nearly as he could determine, would bisect the underground anomaly. He wrote to Holyk on November 4:

> Access routes to the Kidd-55 property [Murray Hendrie Estate] were scouted both on the ground and from the air. T. S. Woolings pulp company has completed cutting [pulp] on Lots 2 and 3 on the north and east boundaries of the Hendrie Estate – their pulp roads form the boundary.
>
> Woolings' roads were found adequate for travel with a muskeg tractor, and so it was not felt necessary to obtain a helicopter for transportation and/or drill camp service.

He then tried to call Edgar Anglehart. Anglehart, a rough, strapping man, had spent a career drifting from mine camp to mine camp. He had been the cook that summer at Texas Gulf's Baffin Island project, but he was also an experienced linecutter and claim staker. Darke liked and trusted him and considered him an exceptionally hard-working and conscientious individual.

Anglehart was traced to North Bay. When Darke reached him by telephone, Anglehart informed him that he had been celebrating with his savings from a summer north of the Arctic Circle and that he now had a touch of stomach flu. Darke gave him instructions to get the next train to Timmins, but Anglehart failed to arrive. After two more days of telephone conversations in which Darke stressed the urgency, he finally proceeded to Timmins, where he stepped across the road from the railroad station and checked into the Empire Hotel.

The next morning he climbed out of bed at dawn feeling very much under the weather. Darke picked him up in the jeep, and the two men made their way north along the emergency service road. Darke led the way through the bush; behind him swayed Anglehart, vomiting along the way.

They spent little more than an hour on the property, chaining off a distance from where Darke had located the approximate boundary line to the point where the grid's baseline would begin. By the end of the day, Anglehart was still shaken but had recovered enough to recruit two friends, Fred Pontello and Guillaume Boudreau, for line-cutting duty. With wide-blade axes, the men cut their way south from the north boundary of the property through 800 feet of water-filled alder and muskeg swamp. It was raining. At right angles to the baseline, Anglehart's crew cut picket lines two or three feet wide at parallel intervals of 100 feet to complete the grid. The entire job took two weeks.

Back in Timmins, Darke put in a call to Holyk, which resulted in Texas Gulf geophysicist Hugh Clayton and assistant Bernard O'Toole boarding a plane for Toronto, and thence to Timmins. Clayton and O'Toole ran an electromagnetic survey along the paths of the grid and reported their observations personally to Darke and to the company's Exploration Manager, Richard D. Mollison:

A massive sulphide-type anomaly extends 700 feet north from the southern boundary. For a further 600 feet, a weak anomaly indicates disseminated sulphides or possibly massive sulphides at depth. In the best portions conductivity is excellent, and the amplitude is at a maximum.

Clayton's memo further reported that the conductor appeared to be 25 feet below the surface of the muskeg at its shallowest depth. Survey results were somewhat contradictory, but it appeared that there were three bands of more highly conductive material running from north to roughly south-southwest, and if that were the case, then there were three widths of possible ore-bearing material, each 50 feet across. If, on the other hand, the three better conductive zones were in fact only integral portions of one conductive band of material, then the width would be more than 300 feet.

Next day, Darke telephoned Canadian Longyear Drilling Company and ordered one drill rig and a crew: one cook, two runners, two helpers to man each of the two 12-hour daily shifts, and a foreman. The foreman, René Gervais, had been a driller when Noranda Mines Ltd. discovered its fabulous Quemont copper orebody in northwestern Quebec during the late 1940s.

The drill crew moved onto the property on November 8, hauling the rig with a small muskeg tractor. It was not common practice to have a drill foreman on a one-rig job, but Darke and his superiors wanted the job pushed. At the same time they decided to skip the added expense of hiring a core grabber, the man assigned to take the tubular core from the drill barrel out of sight from the rest of the crew. This key man marks the core footages, placing the core in shallow, heavy-cardboard coreboxes. Gervais was assigned to act as the core grabber.

Darke located an area in the bush about 200 feet from where the drill was to operate. (Drill camps are often set apart from the anomaly to confuse aerial snoopers, as well as to partially escape the noise of drilling.) Three tents were set up, one for the cook and cookhouse, a second for the four drillers and Gervais, and a third for Darke. The core boxes were to be stored in the third tent.

Then Darke spotted the hole, designated Kidd 55-1. For a while it was known as Dragon 66, a fanciful reference to the Chinese Year of the Dragon, the numeral indicating Texas Gulf's 66th drill probe in the Timmins region. He placed the hole where the geophysical work indicated the earth was shallow, and in a spot where it would make the best test of the ground – it's far cheaper to drill two 500-foot holes than one 1,000-foot hole. The hole was drilled westward at a 60-degree angle so that it would strike through what had been indicated as the three conductive zones. Because of the proximity of the anomaly to the southern and western boundaries of the property, the hole had to be drilled westerly; Texas Gulf had no option on the mineral rights to the neighboring properties, which belonged to a private estate and to the T. S. Woolings Company, a pulpwood subsidiary of the Curtis Publishing Company.

The drill crew spent the early hours of Thursday, November 8, cementing a support around the drill. The support was left to set overnight and on the morning of Friday, November 9, the diamond drill began to churn into the soft earth. Darke went into town late that day and ordered supplies from Marshall-Eccleston Ltd., a Timmins hardware store that outfits bush prospectors.

Late Friday night, Darke, settled into his motel room to plot further work at the property. At 11 o'clock there was a knock, and René Gervais, breathing heavily, thrust forward a muddy length of rock. At a glance Darke could see the glint of copper. He had trouble sleeping that night. He set the alarm for a pre-dawn hour, and timed his departure from the motel so that the jeep would reach the end of the emergency service road at the beginning of daylight. For the next hour, he plodded westward along the muskeg trail toward the site of Kidd 55-1.

Chapter Two

THE INSIDERS BEGIN TO BUY

For most of the hour that it took Ken Darke to reach the Murray Hendrie property from the parked jeep, his thoughts concentrated on Kidd 55-1 and what it might mean for Texas Gulf – and for himself. The day before, René Gervais, the drill foreman, guided by his experience on the Quemont discovery 20 years before, had concluded that this was another rich mine.

Although his hopes were high, Darke was less sure. He had seen only one part of the core, and he knew that this country was abundant with pockets of rich ore which lay in very shallow depths, or else quickly narrowed or "pinched out." Ore deposits frequently occur in variations of an elliptical shape, corresponding to the bottom of shallow ponds or other water basins where the volcanic ash and sediments originally settled millions of years ago.

In fact, Darke had made what he called his first "good pass" in the stock market during the previous month by speculating about the shape and size of an orebody discovered in Ireland by Consolidated Mogul Mines Ltd. The Mogul orebody took the shape of a saucer and lay almost horizontally beneath the surface. As drillers moved from the narrow end of the orebody, Darke gambled that the orebody would continue to deepen into an ellipse, rather than pinching out at a shallow depth. He bought 5,000 Mogul shares on the Toronto Stock Exchange at $2.18 each; as the ellipse widened, Mogal stock rose three months later to $5.50. Darke took a profit of roughly $15,000.

In the light of later events that flowed from Texas Gulf's discovery at Kidd Creek, that $15,000 profit took on an enormous significance for Darke and for many thousands of claimstakers, prospectors, and stock market speculators who eventually rushed to the area. It helped to set off a chain of circumstances which led to an international frenzy in penny mining stocks, the appointment of a Canadian Royal Commission, and revelations without which the United States government might never have laid a case against Texas Gulf Sulphur Company.

It also, incidentally, enabled Darke to become a wealthy man within six months.

Beside the warmth of an oil-burning stove, and with a bucket of water set between his legs, Darke began a systematic visual inspection of the core. The core, lying in rows of five in the 30-inch cardboard boxes, was covered with mud. He submerged each piece in the water bucket to remove the muck, examined it with a hand lens, and replaced it in the box, making sure it was properly labelled. His first entries in a small notebook were:

2 ft	–	sand, boulders
24 ft	–	overburden [clay]
8 ft	–	3% cu [copper]
16 ft	–	traces cu

The next two feet indicated ten per cent copper by weight, and the next 28 feet appeared to be even higher grade. Further down the core, at depths just past 100 feet, Darke ran into evidence of rich zinc ore.

It was dark and eerie by the time he had finished logging the core drilled to that time. During the following two days, drilling was completed to a depth of 655 feet. The bit cut eight feet past the end of the conductor, which just happened to be almost on the boundary of the property that lay to the west. Darke could hear the chatter of the drillers, and although he doesn't speak French, he could sense their excitement. Not wanting to tie up the muskeg tractor, which was equipped with lights and would have made his return so much easier, he made his way on foot towards the jeep. He walked, and where possible ran, along the path. He stumbled through puddles and ponds; his feet were soaked, but it was of no consequence. Despite the darkness, he was back at the jeep within 40 minutes. In daylight the hike took at least an hour.

At the Bon Air Motel, Darke placed a call to Holyk, the chief geologist, at his home in Stamford, Connecticut. Holyk said he would depart for Timmins as early as possible the next day. Holyk in turn called Richard D. Mollison, Texas Gulf's exploration manager, and Mollison called Charles A. Fogarty, then senior vice-president. At the end of this series of conversations it was after 10 p.m. and Fogarty made the decision to rouse President Claude Stephens from his bed with the news.

Much later, an article in *Fortune* magazine reported,

"Though there was manifest excitement, none of the participants recall anything epigrammatic which might mark the moment for posterity."

*

Prior to November 11, 1963, defendant Fogarty owned 705 shares, defendant Mollison owned 50 shares, defendant Clayton [geophysicist Hugh Clayton] owned 200 shares, defendant Huntington [Earl Huntington, an attorney for Texas Gulf] owned 50 shares and defendants O'Neill [Thomas O'Neill, an accountant for Texas Gulf], Darke, Crawford [David M. Crawford, secretary of Texas Gulf], Murray [John A. Murray, office manager for Texas Gulf] owned no shares of defendant Texas Gulf common stock. Prior to that date, none of these individual defendants had ever purchased "calls" [options to purchase] on the shares of defendant Texas Gulf stock.[1]

*

Darke did not return to the property on Monday, November 11, but waited for Holyk's arrival later that day. On Tuesday, the two men were met at the jeep by Gervais, driving the small muskeg tractor. As it jolted along the trail, Holyk remarked that it would be well to hire a larger and more comfortable tractor for the visit of Mollison and Fogarty planned for later that week. Holyk recalled the visit to me as follows:

I flew to Timmins on Monday, Nov. 11, and visited the property on Nov. 12 and logged approximately 600 feet of core with Darke keeping the records. I chained off 2,640 feet from the road on the eastern boundary of the lot in order to determine the approximate location of the

---

[1] From the SEC complaint in the *Joint Appendix, U.S. Court of Appeals — Securities and Exchange Commission vs. Texas Gulf Sulphur Co.*, Vol. 1, p. 81a. The purchases, described on the following pages, may or may not have been a consequence of news of the drilling results.

western boundary of the Royal Trust lot, and was alarmed that the actual boundary was several hundred feet to the east of where Darke had initially pinpointed it. I decided to discontinue further drilling after all the drill rods had been exhausted (which provided for an additional 20 feet of drilling) and thence to dismantle the equipment.

*

Thereafter on November 12, 1963, defendant Fogarty, having knowledge and information of material facts concerning the results of defendant Texas Gulf's drilling on the northeast section, which facts were not generally known by the investing public, purchased 300 shares of defendant Texas Gulf stock at a price of $17⅞ per share on the New York Stock Exchange without disclosing to the seller the aforementioned material facts.[2]

*

Holyk and Darke meanwhile plotted their next moves. Through Gervais, they issued instructions to the drillers that any outside discussions about drill operations were forbidden. It was proposed, and accepted by all but the cook, that the crew would remain on the property at least until Christmas. Their bonus was to be full payment, $1.75 an hour, for a full 12-hour shift every day, even during periods when the drill was not operating.

The next move was the camouflaging of hole Kidd 55-1 and the transfer of the rig to a decoy location. The drill was dismantled and the wooden sills that supported the rig on the mushy surface were lugged from the southwest area of the Murray Hendrie estate to near the northeast boundary. Without leaving the 160-acre property, this was the farthest possible spot from the first hole, and besides it was close to the service road which would provide easy access into Timmins.

---

[2] Ibid., Vol. 1, p. 81a.

There were other considerations: One of International Nickel Company's aerial survey planes had flown directly overhead while Kidd 55-1 was being drilled, and a helicopter belonging to McIntyre-Porcupine Mines Ltd., used to supply and co-ordinate the pulpwood operations of McIntyre had been in the area. The McIntyre chopper was piloted by an acquaintance of Darke's, a man known for his perceptiveness in locating and tracing the activities of ground exploration projects.

To have drilled a second hole near Kidd 55-1 might have led an aerial observer to conclude that Texas Gulf was putting a second drill probe into the same anomaly – a sure sign they were onto something. Darke and Holyk aimed, therefore, to make the deception even more complete; they wanted to make it appear from the air that the site of Kidd 55-1 had never been moved, and that the rig was still operating at the same site.

In accordance with this plan, the second drill site was located in a similar surrounding of trees and brush. The three tents were pitched in the same juxtaposition to each other, and at the same distance from and with the same relationship to the rig. Darke instructed Gervais to burn or bury all wood, paper, and other refuse that had collected around the first drill site. He planted a small tree in the cement collar of the drill casing, and others throughout the site of the first drill hole.

What remained to be obscured were the clearly visible ruts left by the muskeg tractor. From the air the tracks formed a criss-cross network around the first drill site, black pencil lines drawn across a light brown-green terrain. Henceforth, the tractor was not to be driven near Kidd 55-1. As much as possible, the drillers worked to make the tracks indistinct. Pine boughs were scattered over them. Two days later came the first snow of winter, the best possible disguise. The entire area was blanketed in white for the next five months.

On Wednesday, November 13, Darke returned from the property in the early afternoon, and he and Holyk drove to Timmins airport for the expected 4:30 arrival of Mollison and Fogarty. Because of bad weather their plane had been grounded at Sudbury, and they completed their trip by car. The four men waited until early the next day to visit the property.

René Gervais was waiting for them with a larger and more stable muskeg tractor. Still it was a rough ride into the property. Darke and Holyk stood at the back, bracing themselves against a high bar that supports the cargo. Mollison and Fogarty were up front, near Gervais. Darke later described the scene to me: "It was a bumpy ride with numerous detours, through alders, swampy holes and patches of spruce. Everyone had to brace themselves and hang on tightly to prevent being thrown off by the violent gyrations of the muskeg tractor. It was like riding a bucking bronco."

That night, Fogarty, Mollison, and Holyk returned to New York on an evening scheduled flight of Trans-Canada Airlines.

*

Thereafter on November 15, 1963, defendant Fogarty . . . purchased 700 shares of defendant Texas Gulf stock at a price of $17⅝ – ⅞ per share on the New York Stock Exchange . . .

Thereafter on the same day, defendant Mollison . . . purchased 100 shares of defendant Texas Gulf stock at a price of $17⅞ per share on the New York Stock Exchange . . .

Thereafter on the same day, defendant Clayton . . . purchased 200 shares of defendant Texas Gulf stock at a price of $17¾ per share on the New York Stock Exchange . . .[3]

*

---

[3] Ibid., Vol. 1, p. 81a.

The following Sunday, Darke brought back to the camp two bottles of VO whisky and 24 bottles of beer as compensation to the crew for being stuck in the bush. That day, with the authority of Exploration Manager Mollison, he also handed a $250 bonus cheque to Edgar Anglehart. The drill was being established at the second site.

To this date, the evidence of an orebody consisted of one mass of conductive material, detected from the air in 1959, and later confirmed by ground geophysical tests; the rock outcrop containing pinheads of copper lying, apparently, in the same stratigraphic horizon as the conductor; and 655 feet of core which, months later, Darke described as "interesting" but under further prodding admitted was "yes, an excellent core." The only documentary evidence was Darke's and Holyk's rough, pencil-written log of the core. It is well established that any experienced geologist can tell within one-half per cent the copper or zinc content of a piece of rock simply by visual examination.

*

Thereafter, on November 19, 1963, defendant Fogarty . . . purchased 500 shares of defendant Texas Gulf stock at a price of $18⅛ per share on the New York Stock Exchange . . .[4]

*

After discussion on general plans with Holyk and Mollison, Darke pinpointed the location of the second drill hole, knowing that it would bore through worthless rock. The drill crew, ignorant of geophysical surveys which had outlined the conductor, had no way of knowing they were embarked on a futile exercise. It would deceive aerial snoopers, and it would provide lengths of barren core that could be left in full view on the chance a prospector or surveyor or pulpwood worker happened

---

[4] Ibid., Vol. 1, p. 82a.

by. Drill Hole No. 2 – Kidd 55-2 – was started November 20. It was then that Darke faced the first serious crisis, as yet unforeseen in the extensive security precautions. The cook for the drill crew, on the property since November 7, was due to take up duties elsewhere. To have detained the cook would have required some kind of explanation to Canadian Longyear Drilling Company, the cook's employer. After consultation with Holyk and Mollison it was decided that the risk was less by permitting the cook to leave.

*

Thereafter on November 26, 1963, defendant Fogarty . . . purchased 200 shares of defendant Texas Gulf stock at a price of $17¾ per share on the New York Stock Exchange.[5]

Thereafter on November 29, 1963, defendant Holyk . . . caused the purchase by his wife of 50 shares of defendant Texas Gulf stock at a price of $18 per share on the New York Stock Exchange. . . .[6]

*

Edgar Anglehart was assigned to split the core in half, into semicircular lengths. Half of the core was kept in Timmins, the other half sent to Salt Lake City for chemical tests which would confirm, in more precise terms, Darke's and Holyk's visual assays.

By November 30, 1963, Kidd 55-2 was completed, with predictable results. The rig was transported to Prosser Township, which lay diagonally to the northeast of Kidd Township. The drills did not return to Kidd until the end of the following March, by which time the background was set for the case against Texas Gulf Sulphur Company.

---

[5] Ibid., Vol. 1, p. 82a.
[6] Ibid., Vol. 1, p. 83a.

Chapter Three

THE RUMORS BEGIN

Texas Gulf Sulphur Company had developed an extensive security net around operations at Kidd 55, but it wasn't long before holes began to show. In mining, as in the stock market, information can mean money. But even more than that, in Timmins, whose continued existence in a sense depended on the discovery of new mines, there was an acute consciousness of unusual activity in the environs. While it's true that, for once, the magnitude of the Texas Gulf discovery turned out to be such that even rumors tended to be understated, a great many people in the Porcupine mining camp consider the extraction of ore, or the search for new ore, the only suitable topic for discussion.

Mr. Justice Arthur Kelly of the Ontario Supreme Court

was prompted to a discussion of rumors during an investigation into circumstances which arose following announcement of the Texas Gulf discovery. He defined rumors as "current stories passing from one person to another without any known authority for the truth of them," and went on to say:

> There are certain characteristics about rumors and the attitude of people to them. The person who launches the rumor must have some interest in having it circulated; and there must be a probability, or at least a possibility, that it may be true. Also rumors travel faster when the subject matter has importance in the lives of the auditors, and their spread is accelerated when actual news about the matter is either lacking or ambiguous. It is also well known that a desire that it be true will widen its circulation, and that in passing from one person to another, it tends to expand. It may gather authority from the alleged importance of its source and from the character of the person who passes it on. Finally its spread can seldom, if ever, be stopped or slowed down by a simple denial of its truth; and it will die only when it is superseded by an authoritative statement of the facts.

By these criteria, Texas Gulf was particularly susceptible to rumor. And for all practical purposes, it was in no position to issue that "authoritative statement of the facts," which would have been the only certain way to halt the rumor mill.

The first priority of Texas Gulf, one that even took precedence by far over the further investigation of Kidd 55, was the accumulation of land and mineral rights in the surrounding area. It was not simply a case of acquiring land that might contain some geological extension of the Kidd 55 orebody; there was the matter of ensuring that there would be private access to roads and a site for mine plant operations if in fact Texas Gulf had found a commercial orebody. To have announced the results of Kidd 55-1 immediately would have brought mining companies and speculators flooding to the area in a contest for land that would have driven prices upwards. (There have been, at the same time, suggestions that the seller of any piece of property – including land – should in law be made aware by potential purchasers of the intrinsic or potential value of the property.)

Darke, the geologist, and Clayton, the geophysicist, were assigned to marshal the desirable land in the area of Kidd 55. Where land was open for staking under the Ontario Mining Act, they were to proceed by staking; where it was patented land, they were to advise other Texas Gulf officials who were to carry on private negotiations for the acquisition of mineral rights.

While much of the land around Timmins was patented land, for reasons that will be explained later, staking on the scale envisioned by Texas Gulf would require the activity of a large number of people in the field. (By the time the land acquisition program was completed four months later, the company had tied up 60,000 acres.) Negotiations to hire staking teams were by necessity delicate. It would have been desirable to keep each two-man team ignorant of the activities of the others, but of course that was impossible. Among those recruited by Darke were Anglehart and some of his cronies who had helped with line cutting duties on Kidd 55.

Mining claims may be staked by anyone over the age of eighteen who pays $5 to hold a miner's license. But a licensee may not stake more than 18 claims in any one year (April 1 to March 31) in each of the province's 14 mining divisions. Thus there was the need in Texas Gulf's case for several teams of stakers. Claims are squares of roughly 40 acres, and staking requires the erection of four-inch-wide posts at each corner. Boundaries must be marked, either by a trail blazed through the bush, or by pickets or mounds of earth placed at given intervals. Claim stakers frequently get their bearings by using aerial photographs; this staking method later became of importance when a team of stakers working under Edgar Anglehart improperly staked four claims and were required to forfeit them. The claims later fell into the hands of Windfall Oils and Mines Ltd. and became the subject of Canada's greatest mining scandal – a scandal which transformed the nature of the mining industry in Canada.

In order to ascertain which land was open for staking, Darke had to get copies of township maps from the government mining recorder's office in Timmins. He was a frequent visitor there, but it had been his custom to pick up only one or perhaps two maps of the township he was working in. The mining recorder, a slender, orderly young man named Chris Egerton, thought it adequate to meet demand by maintaining an inventory of three maps per township. Darke needed many more than this for his staking program. As casually as possible, he began ordering more maps; to escape suspicion he had Anglehart order further maps. Later, Darke asked Nedo Bragagnolo to pick up maps for him. Bragagnolo, a young real estate salesman who had formerly worked in the mines but quickly tired of working underground, occupied the office on Pine Street next to Darke's. Bragagnolo, too, was to become a millionaire as a result of the Texas Gulf discovery; he is a a shrewd man, and it seems likely in retrospect that his first hint of Darke's clandestine activities was that request to pick up maps at the mining recorder's office down the street.

In early December, 1963, Darke's security precautions began to fail. The drill core from Kidd 55-1 was transported by helicopter from the property to Timmins airport, where it was loaded on a plane. Its destination was an assay office in Salt Lake City.

In the Fountain Court bar of Timmins' main hotel, the Empire, the navigator on these helicopter flights remarked on

THE RUMORS BEGIN   25

the great volume of core that was being flown out of Kidd Township. The Empire Hotel bar is the clearing house in Timmins for all mining intelligence. The helicopter pilot, Doug Boughner, later recalled his own suspicions about the core. On one occasion in early December he had been alone with the core. "They were packed in cardboard boxes, wrapped in burlap, covered with heavy cardboard and bound with wire," Boughner said. "If I could have had just one look at the core I'd be a millionaire today. I'm no geologist, but I know enough to recognize a rich strike when I see one." As far as the rumors went, Boughner was less of a problem than the navigator. He was about to leave the employ of the helicopter firm to work in southern Ontario.

When a reporter from Toronto's *Globe and Mail* phoned Timmins Mayor Leo Del Villano to ask about the rumor that TGS was flying the drill cores to the U.S. for assay in the interest of secrecy, the mayor replied that this would be against the law, because cores had to be kept on the property.

*

Thereafter, on December 11, 1963, defendant Holyk . . . having knowledge and information of material facts concerning the result of defendant Texas Gulf's drilling on the northeast section, which facts were not generally known by the investing public, caused the purchase by his wife of 100 shares of defendant Texas Gulf stock, at a price of $20.37 on the New York Stock Exchange, without disclosing to the seller the aforementioned material facts.[7]

*

It was testimony to the assiduity of the mining grapevine in Timmins that even the forethought of shipping the core as far as Salt Lake City failed to prevent news of the assays from

---

[7] Ibid, Vol. 1, p. 83a.

leaking out. Darke was telephoned one day by an excited Holyk, who began the conversation, "Ken, do you know how much silver was in that core? . . ." Unlike base metals, silver is not easily identifiable by visual assays such as Darke had conducted. Holyk went on to tell Darke that the core had returned silver values higher than 3%.

Somewhat later, Darke was accosted by Mel McCormick, a brokerage salesman of tender age who had recently been hired by the Timmins branch of one of Canada's biggest stockbrokers, Doherty, Roadhouse and McCuaig Brothers. The Doherty, Roadhouse motel office was a few doors from the Texas Gulf office in downtown Timmins, and McCormick and Darke knew each other as acquaintances. McCormick proceeded to repeat to Darke the silver assays that Holyk had reported over the telephone. Darke, trying to hide his shock and anger, pretended to reproach McCormick for his ignorance of mining exploration practice. He told the young salesman that the assays had in fact been repeated to him in a telephone call from New York, but he went on to explain the practice of mining companies in using code names for the transmission of information (. . . it is true that mining companies, when using the telephone or private radio frequencies, use code names to refer to minerals . . .).

"Those figures," said Darke, "refer to barren pyrite [a worthless material commonly found in the Timmins area]." He further suggested to McCormick that he would feel no compunction about laying charges against anyone eavesdropping on his telephone. Darke didn't take any such action, however, even though he shortly learned that McCormick's aunt was an operator at the Timmins telephone exchange.

He called Holyk and said, "Walt, no more telephone talk." Holyk immediately understood, and the two men agreed they would in future exchange all information in writing.

*

Thereafter on December 13, 1963, defendant Mollison
... purchased 100 shares of defendant Texas Gulf stock
at a price of $21.50 on the New York Stock Exchange...

Thereafter on the same day, defendant Holyk . . .
caused the purchase by his wife of calls on (i.e., rights to
acquire) 200 shares of defendant Texas Gulf stock exercisable at a price of $21 per share at any time prior to
June 22, 1964 . . .[8]

Thereafter on December 17, 1963, defendant O'Neill,
having acquired during the course of his employment,
knowledge and information of material facts concerning
the results of defendant Texas Gulf's drilling . . . purchased calls on 100 shares of defendant Texas Gulf stock
exercisable at a price of $21 per share at any time prior
to June 26, 1964. . . .[9]

*

The 655 feet of core brought up from hole Kidd 55-1
contained high mineral values over a length of more than 400
feet. To Darke's practised eye, it was not difficult to identify
the type and approximate quantity of copper and zinc that
was present. He could see the silver also, but he had no idea
how high the values would be. The drillers at Kidd Creek,
too, were experienced at identifying minerals; but in this
instance, they made a curious error. Perhaps influenced by
the fact that International Nickel Company was conducting
an intensive exploration program in the area, and perhaps
because the prospects for nickel were thought to be good in
the geology of the Timmins area, they understood the purplish
streaks in the core to represent a nickel sulphide. They apparently were unaware it was a sphalerite containing zinc.

This came to Darke's attention around Christmastime, when

---

[8] Ibid, Vol. 1, p. 84a.
[9] Ibid, Vol. 1, p. 84a.

strong rumors began circulating in Timmins that Texas Gulf had a major nickel find. The extraordinarily high assay of 10% nickel was frequently mentioned. Darke was telephoned by W. S. Row, the president of Kerr-Addison Gold Mines Ltd., a major producer of gold and other metals. Row made a laughing reference to the rumors of a nickel find, and asked if he could send an emissary. Darke replied that he had no objections.

As Darke recalls it, the Kerr-Addison representative sent by Row came straight to the point and asked if Texas Gulf had found nickel. Darke joked, "Have you ever heard of 10% nickel in these parts?" Then he said, "We have no nickel." It was the truth.

*

Thereafter on December 30, 1963, defendant Fogarty . . . purchased 200 shares of defendant Texas Gulf stock at a price of $22 per share on the New York Stock Exchange . . .

Thereafter on December 31, 1963, defendant Fogarty . . . purchased 100 shares of defendant Texas Gulf stock at a price of $22 per share on the New York Stock Exchange. . . .[10]

*

In its efforts to stop the rumors, Texas Gulf executives made a statement to the *Northern Miner*. On February 27, 1964, the *Miner* reported, "The rumor machine has Texas Gulf obtaining some fat ore indications from its work.

" 'Not so!' was the gist of the remarks of a top T.G.S. executive directly concerned with the company's exploration activities program. . . . T.G.S. has turned up nothing suggestive of an orebody to the moment. But the company is following

---

[10] Ibid, Vol. 1, p. 85a.

up indications of an airborne survey done several years ago. . . ."

*

In the annual report of Texas Gulf Sulphur Company, the opening remark of President Claude Stephens in his message to shareholders was, "Nineteen sixty-three was an eventful year for your company."

Only one paragraph made reference to the company's operations around Timmins:

We have continued our metallic sulphide exploration activities in eastern Canada. The program has included geological and surface geophysical surveys and related drilling, all of which will be intensified during 1964. We have also staked claims on Crown lands and obtained options on patented acreage.

Chapter Four

THE WINDFALL DEBACLE

Viola MacMillan, the Queen Bee of mining. Tough, irascible, inscrutable.

If Viola MacMillan lived in any country other than Canada, with its constant introspection, its lacking sense of history, its inferior self-perspective, she would have been proclaimed in books and plays and song. In mining terms she is Boadicea, Madame Pompadour, and Unsinkable Molly Brown. She has discovered or developed a number of mines, often in places where men have failed. For 21 years she was the president and prime mover of the Prospectors and Developers Association, North America's largest association of mining men.

For 23 days in July of 1964, she held at bay the entire investment community, the Toronto Stock Exchange, and all the forces of persuasion that the Ontario government could muster. Later she went to jail.

Mrs. MacMillan was the promoter of Windfall Oils and Mines Ltd., which had been incorporated (with the more prosaic name, Windward Gold Mines Ltd.) as one of several hundred shoestring exploration companies that sprang up in Canada during the 1940s. She held no formal office with the company, but her husband, George, a soft-featured, white-haired man in his sixties, was the president. The board of directors of the company was composed of an advice-to-the-lovelorn columnist, a farmer who explained his contribution to board meetings by saying, "There has to be a certain number of directors," and others of similarly limited qualifications. Although Windfall had many thousands of shareholders, the directors were all nominees, and they all felt bound to support the views of George and Viola MacMillan.

When Viola MacMillan appeared on the CBS television show "To Tell the Truth" in June, 1964, she and her two impersonators were introduced with these off-camera words:

> I, Viola MacMillan, am president of the Prospectors and Developers Association of Canada. I have been engaged in every phase of the business from grub-staking and swinging a pick to organizing and bringing the mines into production. Among my more successful strikes have been Violamac Mine in Porcupine, Ontario, the Lake Cinch, a uranium mine in Saskatchewan, and Windfall, a property in the Timmins area, adjacent to the recent Texas Gulf Sulphur strike. Over the years, I have discovered and developed mines which, up to now, have produced over $40 million worth of ore.

Viola MacMillan could not claim to have discovered the Texas Gulf mine as she had others, but she was so much a part of the backdrop to the discovery, she so altered the conse-

quences that rippled from it, that despite all her other achievements, her name will always be associated with it.

Only one of the four panel members on "To Tell the Truth"
picked the real Viola MacMillan, and no wonder. She was
110 pounds, not pretty but pleasant, not witty but bright and
vivacious, a woman who by her own admission liked fluffy,
feminine things and going to dances. Viola Rita Huggard was
born in 1903, the thirteenth of 15 children on a farm in the
barren lake country of Muskoka, 100 miles north of Toronto.
Her only association with rocks before her adult years was
when she and a sister drew sand and stones from the family
gravel pit and teamed them down to scows at the lakefront.

High school was out of the question. At 15, Viola moved
to North Bay, Ontario, to live with an older sister, and
attended secretarial school until her money ran out. Now she
was really on her own; she moved to Windsor, just across the
border from Detroit, and while clerking in a store finished her
courses at night in typing and shorthand. Then Viola became
a secretary in a lawyer's office.

It was in Windsor that she met George MacMillan, an
employee in the express department of the Canadian National
Railways in Detroit. George, too, had come from northern
Ontario; he had worked in a mine as a youth, but he had little
interest in mining as a career. He did, however, make use of
his background to become a customer's man in a Windsor
stockbrokerage firm; his specialty was mining stocks. George
and Viola married in October, 1923, when she had barely
turned 18.

In a life as colorful as Viola's, it is hard to separate fact
from legend. There were so many twists of fortune that led
her toward mining. What is true is that George MacMillan's
uncle owned a half interest in two mining claims in northern
Ontario; it is also uncontradicted history that the two young
MacMillans set out in an old jalopy one summer, during their

vacation, to do some assessment work on these claims. It was a lark, really. The claims needed to be worked to remain in good standing, and it was a cheap holiday for George and Viola.

There is no evidence that Viola had the least interest in working on the mining claims. While George was in the bush, she stayed in the town of New Liskeard. "I could have a much better time in town going to dances than tramping through the bush." Notwithstanding, she one day visited a prospector's shack and somehow intervened in a dispute over 200,000 shares of a mining company whose name is long since forgotten. On behalf of two prospectors, she sought help from the Windsor lawyer who had formerly employed her. "I got so excited that I became determined to see it through. I did. I put a chattel mortgage on my furniture to do it, but we won. From then on, mining was in my blood." Whatever the seeds of this story, the modern version may by now be apocryphal; but it serves to illustrate Viola's tenacity, her will to win, and her unwillingness to back away from a fight. More pointedly, it suggests that the attraction mining held for Viola was not in the days spent exploring mining claims, but in the stubborn wheeling and dealing that was just as much a part of mining.

Viola, meantime, started her own real estate business in Windsor. Windsor is the automobile capital of Canada, and in the 1920s real estate was booming. For five summers she and George made their way north, prospecting for gold. They found barely enough in the Porcupine area to pay expenses. When the Depression hit, Viola, still in Windsor, resorted to selling Christmas cards. Her husband took a job with a brokerage firm in nearby London, Ontario, but the happy and reasonably prosperous days of the 1920s were over. According to one chronicle, Viola had been reading everything on mining and geology she could lay her hands on. "I used to go out into the country and just sit there and think. At last

I made up my mind that mining was in the books for me, so I told George I was leaving for the North Friday morning. If he wanted to come along, it would be okay; if he didn't, I'd be all right alone." That last comment denies the close relationship that always existed between them, although there was never any doubt which of the pair made the decisions.

Viola made her first fortune during a staking rush which, like all the others in the Porcupine area, was based on hopes for gold. The MacMillans arrived in Hislop Township north of Kirkland Lake ahead of the main body of prospectors who took part in the staking spree. They picked off 2,000 acres of their own, and then began to organize other claimstakers into syndicates. Viola's claims shortly gave her the biggest single interest in Hallnor gold mine. The MacMillans were rich.

Viola MacMillan was not just an oddity, a woman in the mining business who before she was 30 helped to find a gold mine and got rich in the process. She styled herself the champion of every other independent prospector in the country. She was always against rules or laws which she felt restricted the freedom of prospectors or mine financiers. She started special classes for prospectors and got the government to support them. She went to Ottawa and fought for tax exemptions which allowed mining companies to write off costs of prospecting.

When the Second World War began, Viola was an outspoken patriot. Metals were strategic materials, she preached, and the government and the investing public should be contributing more capital towards their discovery. She organized a National Mining Day. And as a result of all this she was appointed by the federal government to the War Metals Advisory Committee.

George and Viola MacMillan joined the fledgling Prospectors and Developers Association the year after it was formed in 1932. At first she was shunned by her colleagues, but within 12 years she was the association's president: It was all her show, and she turned it into the biggest association of mining men in North America. There was evan a Viola Mac-Millan Ten-Year Plan, designed to make Canada the world's leading mineral producer. All the while she railed at "excessive regulations" – not just those concerning the physical aspects of mining, but also those that governed the raising of money from the public through the sale of shares.

In 1949 Viola raised $40,000 in the stock market to acquire an old group of lead-silver-zinc claims in British Columbia. She turned the property into a major producer. In 1957 she developed a group of valuable uranium claims near Lake Cinch, Saskatchewan. In 1959 she raised $1,000,000 from Lou Chesler, the founder of General Development Corporation, to bring into production the Kam Kotia mine, 14 miles from the site of what was to become the Kidd Creek mine. A year later the MacMillans sold their 42% interest in Violamac Mines, which in turn operated the Kam Kotia mine, for more than $2 million. Viola was having some trouble with her health, and it might have seemed that she and her husband were ready to retire.

In the month before Texas Gulf announced its Kidd Creek discovery, a sign on a tree four miles north of Kidd Township cautioned: "Viola – No Dogs Allowed." The Queen Bee, the Petticoat Prospector, was back in business.

To an interviewer from the *Financial Post*, she said, "I want one more opportunity in mining. The Porcupine is my old stamping ground. This kind of mining exploration is what I like to do. I'm not afraid of the risks and I'm too darn old to change now. I've gotta have another mine." If she found one on those claims she bought from under the nose of Texas Gulf Sulphur she vowed to call it the "Lucky Texas Lady" mine.

The Windfall affair was in a sense an illegitimate offspring of the Texas Gulf discovery. It happened because of a piece of land desired by Texas Gulf but which, through an extra-ordinary series of circumstances, became the property of Windfall Oils and Mines Ltd. The illusion that a worthless piece of land had enormous value was kept alive by the atmosphere that the Kidd Creek discovery created, and because Viola MacMillan, who could have prevented the whole thing from happening, would only say, "I want to be left alone."

The Windfall scandal was a once-in-a-lifetime phenomenon, and it was described as such by the royal commission that spent a year investigating its causes:

> It is hardly conceivable that there should again be such an unusual concurrence of incidents as those which contributed to the market action of Windfall company shares in July of 1964. A remarkable propensity to buy and sell shares of speculative mining companies had grown up in Ontario over the years. This speculative fever, latent but kept alive by great faith in the possibilities of the Timmins area, required something, but not very much, to reactivate it. What was necessary was provided by the remarkable find of copper, zinc and silver made by Texas Gulf. The attention which was focussed on this discovery on the townships north of Timmins was increased by the belief that hidden mineral wealth could not exist in the Texas Gulf orebody without an orebody of comparable value being located in the immediate vicinity. . . .
>
> This caused the public to look upon each property in the area as a potential second Texas Gulf. . . .

Oddly, Viola MacMillan might have in some small way indirectly contributed to the discovery of the Kidd Creek mine. One of the classic occurrences of copper ore in the Porcupine – and one that was diligently studied by the Texas Gulf exploration staff – lay 21 miles west of Timmins at what became the Kam Kotia mine. The mine was configured in a rather small and highly irregular series of orebodies

Big Hollinger Gold Mines Ltd., first acquired the Kam Kotia ground in 1928, did considerable exploration and mined some ore during the Second World War, but decided the economics of the situation didn't warrant further production. Livewire Viola saw further possibilities for the property and acquired it from Hollinger in 1959. Kam Kotia subsequently became a modest but profitable source of copper and zinc.

Kam Kotia had a further significance for Texas Gulf. The April 12, 1964, press release which the Securities and Exchange Commission alleged was "misleading" was drafted with the Kam Kotia orebody in mind. Texas Gulf's optimism in calculating the results of its first four drill holes was tempered by the fact that the Kam Kotia deposit lay in separated and highly varied occurrences of ore. To Exploration Manager Richard D. Mollison this suggested the possibility that Texas Gulf might not have found a unified body of ore, but a potentially much less valuable series of small orebodies.

The four claims that lay in Prosser Township had been marked for acquisition by Texas Gulf because airborne surveys indicated the claims contained conductive material. The anomaly recorded from the air had been a weak one, but the land was considered nevertheless worth exploring further. Some time in the last week of February, 1964, Darke instructed Edgar Anglehart to stake the claims and for guidance in locating the property, he furnished Anglehart with a small aerial photograph marked with the location of the desired claims.

There was a well-defined road running east and west across the aerial photograph. Darke believed this road corresponded to the north boundary of the claims, and marked it as such on the aerial photograph. In fact, the road ran along the south boundary of the claims.

Anglehart, who by this time was staking under contract to Texas Gulf, was set down by helicopter in the vicinity of the property with two assistants. Anglehart fixed the location of the first corner post in accordance with the aerial photograph and left his assistants to complete the staking of the four claims. Two weeks later the claims were recorded in the name of one of the stakers, and in late March they were transferred to the name of Texas Gulf.

Walter Holyk, Texas Gulf's senior geologist, later testified that the conductor that lay beneath those four claims had been detected through the reaction caused by a "third-order anomaly," and therefore was unlikely to indicate the presence of commercial ore. The anomaly at Kidd Creek, in contrast, was of the "first order." Therefore, when Holyk learned the four claims had been improperly staked, he was not unduly concerned. This intelligence, however, was not available to the thousands of speculators who knew only that Windfall had picked up four claims from under Texas Gulf's nose, that the four claims contained some sort of conductor, and that the Texas Gulf orebody lay in a direction which, if extended, ran across the Windfall claims. The Windfall claims, in other words, were "on strike." (This latter is generally interpreted as a sign that the fault in which one orebody occurs may, further down the line, be associated with another orebody. The theory, far from being of value, is highly questionable.)

In the early part of April, at around the time Texas Gulf had resumed drilling its Kidd Creek property, a lumber contractor named Donald McKinnon walked eastward along the north boundary of the claims. He was familiar with the area because of his woodcutting operations. McKinnon became aware that the four claims had not been staked.

After checking with the government mining recorder, McKinnon set out at 7 o'clock the next morning with two friends, John Larche and Fred Rousseau, who had for years been associated in a prospecting partnership. The three men tendered the four claims for recording on April 13, one day after Texas Gulf, in the first press release, described its Kidd Creek property as "merely a prospect," and asked for an inspection order under the Mining Act. Following the inspection, the claims were granted to McKinnon, Larche, and Rousseau.

Texas Gulf took the trouble to telephone the mining recorder and ask if its mistake could be corrected. But that was all. Holyk and Darke had their sights set on the immediate Kidd Creek area, almost four miles away.

Meanwhile, Texas Gulf announced in its April 16 press release that the Kidd Creek property had yielded an orebody of copper, zinc, and silver estimated to contain 25 million tons of ore. That started the land rush. Any land in the general vicinity was the subject of frantic bidding by mining companies and private speculators. The four Prosser Township claims, which in a less feverish atmosphere might have brought $5,000 (Holyk's later estimate) now became worth a fortune in the marketplace.

Enter Viola MacMillan. Viola made preliminary inquiries about the claims, acting on her own personal behalf. She told friends she was "on the verge of a big deal." With Larche, Rousseau, and McKinnon, the MacMillans holed up in a suite in the Empire Hotel to hammer out a deal for the claims. On entering, Viola mentioned to a friend that she was determined not to emerge until she had struck a bargain for the claims.

At 1:30 the next morning the negotiators summoned a lawyer. A contract was signed which provided that Viola would pay $100,000 cash for the claims, along with 250,000 free and negotiable shares of Windfall Oils and Mines Ltd. Windfall shares at the time were selling for less than 40¢. Larche, Rousseau, and McKinnon insisted as part of the deal that the claims be resold to Windfall, because they anticipated (quite accurately, as it turned out) that the claims would enhance the value of Windfall shares.

It was Viola's plan, and one that came close to being successful, to immediately turn around and sell the claims to Windfall for $200,000 cash, 300,000 Windfall shares, and a share of the profits from any mine that might eventuate. If this seems like usury, it apparently did not at the time to the directors of Windfall. A board meeting was quickly convened in Toronto, with Viola present "by invitation," and the deal was approved. Now it required the approval only of the Toronto Stock Exchange, where Windfall shares were listed. "Okay," said Viola, as she strode into the office of stock exchange governor Donald Lawson, "here's what we're going to do."

The stock exchange looked askance at the deal, and over Viola's objections insisted that she sell the claims to Windfall at no more than her cost – and then only when Windfall share-holders had given their approval. Windfall employees were moved onto the Prosser Township claims post haste.

From the beginning the results were disheartening. During the preliminary geophysical surveys, there was difficulty in locating the underground conductor. The length of the cable between the transmitter and the receiver of the survey instrument was increased from 200 to 300 feet – thereby making the instrument more sensitive – and Windfall's consulting geophysicist was finally able to find an appropriate spot for a drill test. Drilling began July 1 and ended four days later at a depth of 570 feet. The stock market hysteria hadn't even begun yet, and virtually all the evidence was in. The conductor turned out to be graphite, a worthless mineral that occurs in abundance near Timmins. (Texas Gulf's Senior Vice-President Fogarty said that his company, after testing the most promising anomalies in the Timmins area, found enough graphite to fill all the pencils of the world for 100 years.)

Whatever rumors were born on the weekend of July 4-5, and there was a rash of them, were later found to be most difficult to trace. The MacMillans, members of the drill firm that had contracted to drill the Prosser Township claims, and others who were privy to whispered conversations, later suffered what was kindly referred to as "a high incidence of amnesia." In any event – and remember that this was after the drill hole had been completed – Windfall shares almost doubled in price on the morning of Monday, July 6, and thereupon rose steadily to a closing price of $1.95.

The events of that weekend, Saturday and Sunday, July 4 and 5, are worth examining because they were built on a foundation of misinformation and misinterpretation and caused a profound change in the public's attitude towards Windfall. The company itself released no information over the weekend, so that the combustive cause of the sudden jump of Windfall shares from 68¢ on Friday to $1 early Monday must have either been spontaneous or the result of deliberately planted rumors.

It began on the Friday, when Nedo Bragagnolo was dining at the Senator Hotel with two of the three men who had sold the Windfall claims to Viola MacMillan. One of the men was called to the telephone and on returning related to his companions a report from Toronto that Bay Street expected Windfall shares to rise once drilling got underway at the company's new property. The report had little substance, but by this time Bragagnolo had become a high roller in the stock market. His companions were no slouches either.

At the property, during the night shift which ended at seven a.m. Saturday, one of the drillers noticed that the sludge around the drill core had turned black. The driller remarked on this to the rest of the crew, saying that he had seen exactly the same phenomenon at another property that had returned good mineral values. The driller, whose name was Boucher, also passed on this information to Edgar Bradley, one of the three owners of the drill contractor firm of Bradley Brothers.

Edgar promptly got on the telephone and relayed this information to his two partners, his brother Wilbert, and Frank Spencer. Some time later that day, John Angus, the manager of a local brokerage firm, heard that Windfall had made a strike.

Meanwhile, George MacMillan arrived at the Windfall property and directed that four boxes of core be placed in his car. Then he visited the office of Bradley Brothers in Timmins to buy some acid: A witness to his visit took it that the acid was going to be used to test the core. MacMillan telephoned his wife in Toronto in the evening, and after midnight, Viola set out by car for Timmins in the company of Ronald Mills, one of the Windfall directors. They drove all night, arriving before seven o'clock Sunday morning.

On Sunday the presumption that Windfall had discovered worthwhile mineral deposits was cross-pollinated among the three principals of the drilling firm. The word spread quickly, and as far away as Noranda, Quebec, the manager of a Noranda brokerage firm was told during a golf game that Windfall had made a strike. The same report reached exploration officials of Noranda Mines, the biggest copper company in Canada.

Spencer and the two Bradley Brothers met to consider the purchase of Windfall shares. They discussed the ethics of buying the shares, since they were at the time retained by Windfall. To resolve this problem, they decided to seek Viola MacMillan's consent to purchase the shares, but they were unable to find her late Sunday. This consent lacking, they decided to act according to their own consciences.

On Monday morning, Windfall shares began trading at $1.01, and during the opening transactions residents of the Noranda-Rouyn area of Quebec bought a total of 111,200 shares. Stockbrokers acting for these buyers purchased for their own accounts – and for the accounts of other clients –

another 74,500 shares. Among these buyers were all three partners of the Bradley Brothers firm and an exploration official of Noranda Mines. Although broker-client relationships are supposed to be confidential, the investment community in Toronto was soon rife with rumors that buyers of Windfall stock included the principals of the very contracting firm that was drilling the Windfall property. What better indication could there be that Windfall had a find? In addition, the very fact that the stock was rising was proof to many speculators that there had been a discovery.

Judge Kelly later attributed that sudden rise to events of the weekend, "the effect of which was heightened by the atmosphere prevailing at the time. . . ." He continued:

> The discovery by Texas Gulf had whetted the public's desire to risk money in a type of gamble which returned large rewards to the winner. This, and confidence that some other mineral deposit must be present close to such a remarkable ore body as that which Texas Gulf had discovered, ensured ready acceptance of the belief that another mine was at the point of discovery. Everyone wanted another discovery, and was anxiously looking for any sign which would give early indication of the expected find.

Ken Darke, aware that there was scant evidence of an orebody on the Prosser claims, at least from aerial surveys, was not caught up in the buying fever. On July 6, when the market went wild, Darke sold short 5,000 Windfall shares. He continued to sell short as the stock's price ranged around $2, and by July 9 he was short 45,000 shares. At that stage he stood to make a lot of money.

Viola MacMillan was also a big seller of Windfall shares, but unlike Darke she was working on a sure thing. Concurrent with the sale of the property to Windfall, she had agreed to buy one million shares from Windfall's treasury at prices ranging from 40¢ up to 70¢. This system of "primary distribution" on the Toronto Stock Exchange has been perhaps the biggest reason that the Toronto Stock Exchange, until the Windfall affair, was the world's busiest stock market in shares of speculative mining stocks. Viola was committed to buy only 100,000 shares at 40¢; thereafter, she was free to purchase or ignore the remaining 900,000 shares. As it turned out, she profited to the extent of $1,400,000 on this wholesale-retail operation.

Ken Darke, in contrast, the man whose skill had helped to discover the Kidd Creek orebody, one of the few people who had meaningful information about Windfall's Prosser Township claims, lost $129,631.89.

To speculators and prospective speculators in Windfall shares it became imperative to learn the results from the first drill core. But George and Viola MacMillan remained inaccessible to the press, and to those they couldn't help but encounter in their day-to-day affairs they were equivocal at best. Certainly they did nothing to short-circuit the false rumors about the presence of mineral values in Windfall's core. In fact on Thursday, July 9, George MacMillan told James Scott, Business Edtior of the *Globe and Mail*, "If you want to be poor all your life, don't buy Windfall."

It came out much later that on the morning of July 6, Mrs. MacMillan had taken two small pieces of near-surface drill core to the Technical Service Laboratory in Toronto for assay. Later that day she was informed by telephone that the results showed nothing of value. That same day, George MacMillan supplied consulting geologist Dr. J. W. Ambrose with samples of the core. He examined them but did no assays and eight days later informed Viola MacMillan that he had been unable to detect anything of commercial value.

One other man was almost certain that Windfall had nothing.

Geologist Patrick Heenan, acting for Conwest Mines, chartered a helicopter on July 6 and flew to the Windfall drilling site. There was no one present when he arrived so he removed some of the sludge from the drill collar and immediately returned to Timmins and had the sample analysed. The next morning he had the report – there were no minerals present. Heenan informed his own company of his discovery but told no one else.

On July 10 Windfall rose to a new high of $4 per share, partly because Ken Darke had begun to worry and had become a big buyer. For one thing, Roy Powley, a garage operator in Timmins, reported to Darke that George MacMillan had said that the drill core contained mineralization. Darke checked further with an owner of the drill contracting firm that had been retained by Windfall; he remembers being told that the drilling gave evidence of a copper find. Darke, who had sold 45,000 Windfall shares he did not own, reversed his field and in one day bought 70,000 shares.

The following weekend, reporters for the weekly *Northern Miner* frustrated like other newspapermen in their efforts to contact the MacMillans, turned ingeniously to Mr. Wardrope, the Ontario Minister of Mines. One of the *Miner*'s editors recalled that Wardrope gave him an optimistic account of Windfall's findings; Wardrope later recalled saying no such thing. Whatever was the nature of that conversation, Wardrope was not in the habit of dashing cold water on hopes that new mineral wealth would be found in his province.

In an editorial, the *Northern Miner* congratulated the MacMillans for their apparent new and significant discovery:

> Although the full significance of it is not known as this is being written, the fact remains that Windfall Oils and Mines has apparently come up with a promising metals discovery. . . .

For this, congratulations are due the Mining Mac-Millans – vivacious and colorful Viola, quiet and competent George . . .

They moved into the area with great fortitude, paying a huge price for a prime piece of property.

It was a big gamble, in some respects, but it was also an intelligent gamble, based on what ultimately proved to be the right interpretation of the very little technical data available at the time. . . .

The *New York Herald Tribune*, meanwhile, ran a three-column story with the headline (mercifully followed by a question mark), "New Canadian Bonanza? Windfall Stirs Investors." According to the *Herald Tribune* story, the Mac-Millans had "stunned the speculative market" by pulling "a major base metal drill core."

But the Windfall affair was getting out of hand. Not only did the public deserve some kind of disclosure, but many people within the investment community, the stock exchange, and the government had too much at stake to risk further without prying some information from the MacMillans. On July 10 a telegram went out from the Toronto Stock Exchange to Windfall carrying the ultimatum that if "an up-to-date statement . . . satisfactory to the exchange" were not delivered over the weekend, Windfall shares would be suspended from trading.

Other developments were taking place which not only failed to enlighten, but also ripened the curiosity of people with an intense interest in Windfall's stock market fate. Nedo Bragagnolo had a large stake in the shares, and in the company of a stock promoter and two reporters from the *Northern Miner* decided to make his own attempt at prying information out of Viola MacMillan. He invited Viola to visit a property owned by one of his own companies where he had just pulled what he called an "interesting" drill core. By showing Viola this core, Bragagnola hoped she would be inclined to reciprocate. He was wrong. Viola responded by quoting lines from Rudyard Kipling's poem, "If." With the stock promoter and the two reporters he rushed back to Timmins, searched for a book that included the poem, and studied it word for word. They concentrated on the stanza Viola had quoted:

If you can talk with crowds and keep your virtue,
Or walk with kings – nor lose the common touch,
If neither foes nor losing friends can hurt you,
If all men count with you but not too much,
If you can fill the unforgiving minute,
With sixty seconds worth of distance run,
Yours is the earth and everything that's in it,
Which is more – you'll be a man, my son.

Bragagnolo and his friends sought in vain for some clue, some hidden meaning. They finally decided it was futile to probe into the mind of Viola MacMillan.

The statement from Windfall did not arrive at the Toronto Stock Exchange by the deadline, but trading in the stock was nevertheless permitted to continue at the opening on Monday, July 13. The chairman of the stock exchange explained later that a decision to carry out the threat of suspension would have constituted "a very severe penalty to shareholders."

The statement from Windfall arrived later that day, and it was anything but satisfactory. It said that drilling had been stopped on the first hole at a depth of 530 feet and that no core samples had yet been sent for assays. This was technically correct: The core had not been chemically assayed, but it was a fact that at least George MacMillan had seen the core. And numerous geologists testified subsequently that one glance at the core would have made it clear to anyone with even limited mining experience that neither copper nor zinc were present in commercial quantities. Implicit in the Windfall statement was the suggestion that core drilling could not be continued until security precautions were taken. "Facilities for protecting and dealing with core have been lacking and the unexpected (public) interest has made a suitable core shack essential." The statement also referred to "snoopers trying to get information off the property." It concluded: "Further work will be advanced according to mining procedure appropriate for the development of what is hoped will prove to be worthwhile properties."

It was abundantly clear that stronger measures would be needed to prompt Windfall to disclose some hard facts. The Ontario government exerted its authority and convened a meeting of the MacMillans, representatives of the Ontario Securities Commission and the Toronto Stock Exchange. Windfall shares were trading at about $4.

What happened at that three-hour meeting must rank as one of the most embarrassing incidents in the history of Ontario's attempt to regulate securities markets.

Viola made mincemeat of her adversaries. She told the chairman of the securities commission that an attempt to force Windfall to disclose information would be "a stone around his neck the rest of his life." The MacMillans took the position that it would be against mining practice to make known results until the drill hole was "completed." (The hole was already at the depth recommended by Windfall's consulting geophysicist.) In defence of her stand, Viola was later recalled to have said, "This is like wildfire; release of information would make it a holocaust." That was one of the instances where, according to the recollections of the participants, the MacMillans "gave you lots of opportunities to think there was something quite valuable there."

The Ontario Securities Commission thereupon issued its own public statement, which perpetuated the myth that Windfall had found something of value "To lessen the possibility of rumors . . . all cores will be under guard," and "No information will be released by the company in regard to the cores until the assays are completed," which had the effect of giving the Ontario government's sanction to the vacuum of disclosure which surrounded Windfall.

If it seemed the government was by now conspiring with the MacMillans to maintain the Windfall silence, there was even more to it than that. The director of the Ontario Securities Commission, John Campbell, who under the policy supervision of the chairman administered the day-to-day operation of stock-policing activities in Ontario, had with his wife, a one-time model and movie starlet, developed a social relationship with the MacMillans. The Campbells at this time were financially squeezed and Mrs. Campbell tried to make some money in the market.

At first John Campbell was not aware that his wife, Bunty, had purchased Windfall shares on the advice of Viola Mac-Millan. He redressed the problem by arranging for the sale of the stock. Later, when trading in Windfall shares reached its fever pitch, Mrs. Campbell sold short. However, such was the volume of buying of Windfall shares, she was unable to secure stock to make delivery against her short sale. Mr. Campbell again came to the rescue by borrowing – from Viola Mac-Millan – 5,000 Windfall shares.

The nature of John Campbell's personal affairs may not have been influenced by his dogged but unsuccessful efforts to persuade the MacMillans to provide information of the drill core. At times during that month of July, it seemed that Campbell was working against his own best personal interests. For example, he fought against the suspension of Windfall shares, even though suspension would surely have the effect of depressing the price and rendering his wife's short sales highly profitable. It was almost inadvertent, then, that the

Campbells profited to the tune of almost $30,000 when the Windfall bubble burst.

In one instance at least, John Campbell did show his friendly relationship toward the MacMillans. He phoned Mines Minister George Wardrope to enlist his help in the MacMillans' case. As Wardrope later described it:

"On July 11th, 1964, I was called at my home in Port Arthur by Mr. Campbell, who asked when I would be returning to Toronto. I told him that I would be on the plane the following afternoon, and I agreed to meet him and Mr. and Mrs. MacMillan that evening as he requested. The reason he gave for asking me to meet them was that he and the MacMillans did not understand precisely what information the Toronto Stock Exchange required concerning Windfall. He said he believed that I, as a long-time acquaintance of General Graham [president of the Toronto Stock Exchange], might be able to get from him a definite statement of the requirements. In view of the fact that the Toronto Stock Exchange had indicated concern over the activity of Windfall stock about which no information was being made available to the public, I was glad to do anything that I properly could do to straighten out the situation.

I tried to contact the Honorable Mr. Wishart, the Attorney-General, to ask him to accompany me to the meeting, but he was away from the city. For similar reasons it was not possible to get a number of other officials . . . . Finally, I reached the Mine Assessor and Comptroller of the Department of Mines, Mr. B. C. Lee, who met me with the others in my room at the Royal York Hotel. During the meeting I called Mr. W. B. Common, the then deputy attorney-general, and explained to him the gist of the meeting.

In the presence of Mr. and Mrs. MacMillan, Mr.

Campbell, and Mr. Lee, I telephoned General Graham to ask exactly what additional information was required to make the statement on the position of Windfall acceptable to the Stock Exchange. During the conversation I made several rough notes of General Graham's observations and passed the information on to Mr. and Mrs. MacMillan so that they might prepare a revised statement to the Stock Exchange. The rough notes I made during the conversation with General Graham were given to the MacMillans when they retired to draft their amended statement to the Stock Exchange.

The gist of General Graham's message as I received it from him over the telephone was that if a satisfactory statement on Windfall were in his hands by 10:30 the following morning it would be submitted to the Board of Directors of the Toronto Stock Exchange for consideration.

I called General Graham again shortly after 10:30 a.m. the next day (July 13th) to ask if he had received the statement. His answer was "no."

I then called Mr. Campbell and was told by him that, before being presented to the Exchange, the statement would have to be approved by Windfall's secretary, Mr. Cole, who was at his summer cottage and temporarily isolated because of a storm. He expected it would be possible to reach him early in the afternoon. I called General Graham again to relay this information to him.

Although the Ontario Securities Commission and the Toronto Stock Exchange had issued a public reprieve for Windfall in the middle of July, private efforts were continued to hasten the disclosure of assay results. Public speculation was unabated, and the price of Windfall reached its high of $5.65 on July 21.

Even Texas Gulf couldn't contain its curiosity, and moved

a drill rig onto land adjoining the Windfall claims. Needless to say, this heightened the widely held conviction that Windfall had positive evidence of a mine.

The stock market excitement had become so great that even persons who never gambled in the penny dreadfuls of the mining market were being touted on Windfall. On July 25 I was phoned by Jack Salloway, a customer's man at the respected firm of Greenshields & Co., who said that "I have it straight and confidentially from the man who is Viola's closest friend. Windfall's results are unbelievably rich – 93 feet of over 10% copper. You have to buy." I rarely buy penny stocks; the risk is too high and the gamble too great and I am not basically a happy gambler, but it was very difficult to resist this "inside" information. In addition I knew that Jack Salloway would not deliberately mislead me, for I had looked after his family medically from the time he married.

Looking back I realize how very lucky I was, for under those strange circumstances it would have been very easy to become deeply involved.

If the patience of speculators was being stretched, it was not apparent from the price of Windfall shares. July 30 was set as the date for release of assays, and on that day Windfall shares rose $1.05 to $4.10. That night after the market closed, Windfall directors received the assay results and released them to the public.

What the assay revealed was "copper mineralization . . . throughout the drill core" but nothing approaching the proportions that could suggest the presence of a mine. I received the news by phone at 10 p.m. from Al Dow, a close friend and a financial reporter at the *Toronto Star*. I found it difficult to believe.

The next morning there were no buyers, and trading in the stock was delayed. There was pandemonium on the floor of the Toronto Stock Exchange. Exchange officials managed to form an ad hoc consortium of member firms who entered bids at 80¢, enabling trading to begin. Shortly afterwards, Windfall shares were trading below 40¢ – the same price as when the hysteria began.

Very few people came out of the Windfall affair with honor. The Ontario Securities Commission and the Toronto Stock Exchange were discredited. John Campbell was charged with breach of trust of his duties as Securities Commission director. Viola MacMillan was charged and found guilty of wash trading – manipulating the price of a company's shares by artificially creating the appearance of trading activity. A more lasting result was that the promotion of mining stocks in Ontario, and to a lesser extent elsewhere in Canada, was severely restricted, and that mining professionals began to question the responsibilities of geologists and the publicly accepted definitions of such vague phrases as "proven" and "probable" ore reserves, "mineralization" and even "ore."

Thousands of speculators who had never owned stock in Windfall lost money as a result of the Windfall disaster, for its collapse triggered the fall of many other speculative mining companies who had been searching for ore in the Timmins area. On October 14, 1965, the *Northern Miner* described the sad scene:

What's the matter with the Toronto mining market, Bay Street was asking itself this week? With the big N.Y. board at an all-time high and the whole Canadian economy zooming along at an unprecedented clip, all indices on the T.S.E. gave up ground. It was a rather odd anomaly. Among mines, new lows outnumbered new highs 3-to-1. To the man on the street (and he's probably right) blame for the T.S.E. malady stems back to the Windfall fiasco, which came to light again this week with some shocking headlines. The revelations brought to light by the Kelly Royal Commission report certainly puts the T.S.E. in a dim light as far as the public is concerned. "What with 'insider' market shenanigans, the type of mine financing in which the broker and underwriter simply can't lose, undeclared short selling, etc., etc., I'm just fed up," a pretty level headed (and successful) trader remarked to the Northern Miner this week.

One aspect the *Northern Miner* story didn't mention was the involvement of persons at the *Miner* itself in the trading of Windfall shares. On July 2, when Windfall was 62¢, Graham Ackerley, the *Miner* reporter who was writing the Windfall story, first purchased shares of Windfall on the suggestion of Mrs. MacMillan. He ended up making a little over $1,000. Maurice Brown, the senior assistant editor of the *Miner*, purchased 2,000 shares of Windfall on July 8, the day before the *Miner* carried their front page Windfall story. In total he purchased 14,000 shares and made $4,450. Richard Pearce, president and general manager of the *Northern Miner*, purchased 2,000 shares on July 6 at $1.72 and resold them one week later at $2.70.

In the 1964 Windfall inquiry the following devastating exchange took place:

Q: Mr. Brown, from your experience is it a fact that stories in the paper, in your paper, influence the market?

A: Sometimes, yes.

Q: Is there any policy on your paper, Mr. Brown, with regards to purchasing shares in companies about which you write?

A: We have two basic rules: We must not sell a stock short; and we cannot take a call on stock. Otherwise I would say there is no – except they expect us to use discretion.

It is hard to believe, but the *Northern Miner* not only does not prohibit stock trading by its employees in issues they are reporting – it does not even require disclosures of such purchases to its readers! When I related this to an official at Reuters, the news agency that transmits crop and other financial news, he was amazed, and pointed out the employees of Reuters must sign a pledge agreeing never to trade in any security which they are reporting.

The *Wall Street Journal* goes even further. Their employee instructions read:

> We require our staff members to bend over backwards to avoid any action, no matter how well intentioned, that could provide grounds even for suspicion that he made financial gains acting on the basis of inside information obtained through his position on our staff before it was available to the general public. Such information includes hold for release material and our plans for running exclusive interviews and other stories that may affect price movements. . . .
>
> Because we consider it so essential that every member of our staff be above suspicion, we consider any slip in judgment in this area serious enough to warrant dismissal.

Mines Minister George Wardrope was given a rough time while the rumor mills worked overtime. During his tenure as Mines Minister, Mr. Wardrope had a reputation among reporters in the Queen's Park press gallery as an easy mark, who could never say no to a plea or request. As Mr. Wardrope later recalled, he said he was called into the office of Ontario Prime Minister John Robarts, who asked, "Are you involved?"

"I said, 'John, I haven't bought any shares in anything since I came into politics 16 years ago – I haven't got a nickel in this and the only thing that worries me is what it is going to do to the name of mining."

Mr. Robarts replied, "We're going to have to stand a lot of gaff on this but now that I have your word, I'm not worried."

The royal commission inquiry into the activities of Windfall Oils and Mines Ltd. on the Toronto Stock Exchange ultimately cleared Mr. Wardrope of any connection with the scandal.

Many other innocent people were affected.

Viola MacMillan had been president of the Prospectors and Developers Association for 21 years, during which time she had turned it into an education forum for mining men, a significant lobbying force, and an estimable focus for the high society of government and mining. When Windfall shares flopped, the association almost did the same.

Viola resigned the presidency of the association shortly after the Windfall stock market fiasco. "As you know," she said in her letter of resignation, "criticism has been directed at me by a few members of this association, criticism which unfortunately I am not in a position to answer at this time." Viola's withdrawal brought about the cancellation of that year's annual four-day convention at Toronto's Royal York Hotel. Two thousand people had booked more than 400 rooms at an affair which annually brought $200,000 worth of tourist business to Toronto.

The *Northern Miner*, which had previously heralded the Windfall "discovery" ran a front page editorial with the headline, "A Black Day for Canadian Mining." The President of the Toronto Stock Exchange, in a masterpiece of understatement, called it "odd that this aura of mystery has surrounded this thing." Maybe John Campbell knew better than anyone why Viola MacMillan had succeeded in maintaining silence while thousands of members of the public were deluded into speculating about a worthless piece of property in the northern bush. Campbell's explanation of his inability to obtain information from Viola MacMillan was, "You just don't go to Viola and say, 'I want this,' or 'we are going to do this.' I mean, you just don't do that to Viola MacMillan."

To my great surprise, I was personally to have one further unpleasant involvement with the aftermath of the Windfall collapse.

Viola MacMillan was convicted of wash trading in the shares of Consolidated Golden Arrow Mines and she was sentenced to an indeterminate term of nine months. However, after serving only seven weeks of her sentence, she was released on parole. This quick release disturbed many who felt that she had been given special treatment because of her wealth, and there were several ill-tempered arguments in the legislature as a result. The Minister of Reform Institutions blandly insisted that Mrs. MacMillan's case had been "handled in exactly the same way as any other inmate's case." I did not take any part in these debates.

On April 6, 1968, together with Pat Lawlor, another member of the legislature, I toured Mercer Reformatory for Women. With amazement we read on the bulletin board for inmates: "If you have other charges outstanding, it is best to get them cleared up as soon as possible because you cannot be given parole while another charge is outstanding." This was attributed to a speech given to the inmates by Mr. Frank Potts, Chairman of the Ontario Board of Parole.

Inasmuch as Mrs. MacMillan still faced a joint charge of fraud with her husband, George, arising out of share dealings in Windfall, we immediately concluded that she had indeed received very special treatment. We released a statement: "It is intolerable that there should be different rules for the rich and the poor in this province. Furthermore it is shocking that Reforms Institution Minister, Allan Grossmann, was not aware of this matter when he told the legislature that parole could be granted a person facing a charge." The next day, government officials said it was all a mistake and that the bulletin board should have read, ". . . you may not be given parole while another charge is outstanding."

Two days later I was amazed to read the headline of the *Toronto Telegram*:

SHULMAN BLASTED: VIOLA HAD HEART RELAPSE.

Viola MacMillan's minister accused Dr. Morton Shulman (NDP, High Park) of persecuting the millionaire mining promoter following her parole after serving seven weeks of a nine-month sentence for stock manipulation.

Rev. Arthur D. Brown, of St. Michaels and All Angels Church, said in an open letter that Dr. Shulman's accusations of discriminatory treatment in favor of Mrs. MacMillan by the Department of Reform Institutions were unfair.

Mr. Brown said Mrs. MacMillan suffered aggravation of a heart condition while she was in jail. . . . "There are other factors for paroling a person besides wealth – the nature of the misdemeanor, age and physical and mental health, the contribution a person has made to society, adjustment to correctional treatment and the chance of a complete rehabilitation, the contribution one can make to society after incarceration, the length of time when sufficient debt to society has been discharged."

Another mitigating factor was that she had made a contribution to society equalled by few people, he said.

"I am not arguing as to whether she has made mistakes or not." Mr. Brown's letter said.

"I am concerned that she not be persecuted by a slanted political opposition and that she have opportunity for a fair trial by the judiciary and the public."

Reverend Brown did not limit his help to Viola MacMillan to intervention with God and the *Telegram*. He also approached Kelso Roberts, Attorney General of Ontario until 1962, and persuaded him to join the team of lawyers managing the MacMillan defense.

On February 10, 1969, Viola MacMillan was acquitted of the charges of fraud laid against her in connection with trading in the shares of Windfall. The Toronto press described the scene thusly:

"I just can't believe it, I just can't believe it," cried Mrs. MacMillan, 66, as the verdict was announced.

Mrs. MacMillan, wearing a neat burgundy-colored suit, and a chic mauve hat sat beside her white-haired husband, George, 69, in the prisoner's box as County Court Judge Harry Deyman crisply read his judgment.

As the judge finished, Viola turned to her husband and smiled.

Then both left the box to be congratulated by the three lawyers who have defended them during their three-week trial – Joseph Sedgwick, John J. Robinette and former attorney-general Kelso Roberts.

Judge Harry Deyman said he could find no evidence that they had affected the public market price of the stock or that they had falsely promoted the sale of stock.

The judge said the mining sites where the MacMillans were drilling in the Timmins area were close to the Texas Gulf discovery. The stock of Windfall Oils and Mines jumped from 56 cents July 3, 1964 to $1.01 on July 6.

Judge Deyman said this jump was the result of a lot of buy orders from the Timmins area over the weekend but he added that Mrs. MacMillan had been reluctant to put extra shares on the market at that time.

In connection with a second charge of fraud through the promotion and sale of the stock, Judge Deyman said the Crown had alleged that the MacMillans did nothing to deny rumors about the value of the mine.

But the judge said he could not find anything fraudulent in the MacMillans' press release or in their statements to the press. "There was nothing said that wasn't factual."

Judge Deyman said an independent geologist described the mining site as "an interesting piece of property." He added that the drill core was interesting to professional people and that the prospectors who sold the site to Mrs. MacMillan were also interested by the property.

Describing Mr. MacMillan as an experienced prospector, the judge said that he didn't mislead anyone.

"The delay in having the drill core assayed was not fraud," he said.

Judge Deyman also said he did not think the Mac-Millans were wrong in waiting until a drill hole on the Windfall property was finished before releasing a drill report.

*

Court of Appeals Justice Mr. Arthur Kelly, who conducted the hearings into trading of Windfall shares, had come to somewhat different conclusions than did Judge Deyman:

> "It is impossible to believe that a person having the knowledge and experience of George MacMillan could have made even a cursory examination of the drill core and continued to believe it contained copper and zinc in percentages to be considered commercial. . . . Many people who entered the market after July 7 suffered losses through the complete failure of George and Viola Mac-Millan, as officers and controlling shareholders of a company, to recognize their obligation to see that trading of the shares of the company on a public exchange took place in the light of the most accurate information available and without any misinformation capable of correction which had a direct bearing on the market price. . . . Not only did they refrain from telling the truth, but in such statements as were made, the facts which were stated and the manner in which they were framed were

such as to be misleading and must have been calculated
so to be."

*

At the close of his 13-page decision, Judge Deyman
quietly asked the MacMillans to stand and said:

"I must find you not guilty on both counts. You are
discharged."

A happy Mrs. MacMillan posed for photographers
and said, "We're just glad it's over. It's been almost five
years now.

"We always felt we were not guilty but it is nice to have
the judge clear us."

Mr. MacMillan said: "Once we got into court it wasn't
as much of a strain because it was interesting. The hard
part was waiting for the case to come to a head."

His wife said that mining has been their life and that
they have always been interested in it. Now that the case
is over they can go back and concentrate on business, she
said.

Windfall is still an active company. Mr. MacMillan
said there had been drilling done on their site near
Timmins last year. He shrugged and indicated they feel
they might find an ore body there.

Crown counsel Rod Cormack said today that while the
attorney-general's department has 30 days in which to
decide whether to appeal the acquittal, "as far as I am
concerned, this is it – there will be no appeal."

It is estimated that the MacMillans made a profit of $1
million in the trading of the shares of Windfall.

Mrs. MacMillan had the last word on the subject. On June
25, 1969, she was quoted, "It's so sad all this had to last five
years. There are so many great Canadians and I consider
myself one of them. I'm a great developer."

Chapter Five

TEXAS GULF: THE LEGACY OF BERNARD BARUCH

In one of those instances where history appears to turn full cycle, Texas Gulf Sulphur Company Inc. was born of the kind of frenzied frontier migration that almost 50 years later the company itself helped to create. In both instances two elements were present: The frontier ethic that makes possession of land an asset beyond the real value of that land; and, however irrational, the widespread belief that newfound wealth is a contagious commodity.

Texas Gulf came to life as a consequence of the fevered search for oil at the turn of the century on the Gulf Coast. Its early years were inauspicious, even neglectful. And when the First World War made the supply of sulphur a matter of national contingency, Texas Gulf, despite hurried preparations, arrived too late as a major producer. In Texas in the early 1900s, as many people were disappointed in the search for oil as in Timmins in the early 1960s were left with shares of worthless muskeg.

Sulphur had become worthy of extraction from the Gulf Coast in 1891, when a German-born petroleum engineer, Herman Frasch, devised a method of recovering sulphur with hot water. Five years later Frasch established his Union Sulphur Company. The Frasch technique, however practical (Texas Gulf still uses variations of it), remained under patent until 1908. Until that time, then, and even afterwards, the chunks of sulphur-bearing rock that blew from the oil rigs were no less a blighted hope than the pieces of mud that accompanied them.

During the Texas rush, numerous oil prospectors had tested the Big Hill salt dome in Matagorda County and found it wanting. An early group of prospectors forming what was known as the Cash-Mayes syndicate drilled the Big Hill dome as early as 1901, but abandoned the area after three holes. Another syndicate drilled a fourth hole on the formation, and although they found a 93-foot stratum of sulphur-bearing limestone – the first real discovery of sulphur on the Big Hill dome, it went almost ignored because of their preoccupation with the search for oil.

A further 30 or so wells were drilled there, and the Big Hill became for a time a modest source of oil. But when the Humble Oil field was discovered in 1904, north of Houston, the Big Hill was all but deserted.

In 1908, concurrent with the expiry of Frasch's basic patent, two St. Louis businessmen, A. C. Einstein and John W. Harrison, arrived in Texas to drill for sulphur. They promptly obtained rights to the Big Hill dome which had previously been held by the prospecting syndicates. Exploratory drilling turned up more quantities of sulphur-bearing limestone, and with businessmen from nearby Texas communities, Einstein and Harrison organized the Gulf Sulphur Company on December 23, 1909. That was the beginning.

The Gulf Sulphur Company was a very limited concern in the next few years. Until 1916 its activities were confined to exploration and the acquisition of more land. Production was too costly a venture, the sulphur market was already adequately supplied, and anyway the Gulf Sulphur group was not financially competent to go into production.

In 1916 Bernard Baruch came to Big Hill with his consultant, Seeley Mudd. Mudd had earlier scouted the Gulf Coast for sulphur prospects and Baruch had in fact engaged in earlier talks with Gulf Sulphur. Now to Baruch the time seemed ripe for the development of the Big Hill.

With Baruch as the prime mover, the J. P. Morgan partnership bought about 60% of Gulf Sulphur; William Boyce Thompson, a Canadian resources financier, took the rest. Mudd was appointed president and Gulf Sulphur was renamed Texas Gulf Sulphur Company in 1918.

The United States' entry into the war in November, 1917, substantially altered the plans for the Morgan-Thompson interests. Baruch's attentions were diverted when he was appointed by President Woodrow Wilson to the War Industries Board. Mudd, commissioned an officer, also joined the war effort.

Mudd's withdrawal left the presidency open. As his successor, Boyce Thompson determined upon a 51-year-old engineer with a brilliant technical mind, Walter H. Aldridge. This appointment set the course of Texas Gulf's fortunes for the next 38 years. It was an era during which Texas Gulf asserted itself as the world's largest and lowest-cost sulphur producer; Aldridge's reign was also characterized by a stubborn adherence to a narrow path which kept Texas Gulf wholly reliant on the vicissitudes of the market for that one commodity until the 1960s.

Because of demands made by the war, Washington encouraged Texas Gulf and other sulphur companies to enlarge production plans. But the company needed priority rights to acquire equipment and supplies that were in short supply. Although the official history of Texas Gulf takes pains to point out that Bernard Baruch steered clear of the company's affairs because of his financial stake, it is difficult to imagine that his presence on the War Industries Board did not favor Texas Gulf. Although the company as yet was not a producer and therefore had no contracts, priorities for the supply of materials were issued by the government in the summer of 1918.

Construction of a plant built around 14 702-horsepower boilers took eight months. During that period Texas Gulf drilled another 20 development wells and outlined a thick, elliptical sulphur-bearing formation underlying about 300 acres of Big Hill dome. On March 1, 1919, the boilers were fired, and Texas Gulf produced its first sulphur the next day.

Aldridge's ingenuity was about to be tested. The armistice had preceded Texas Gulf's first production by four months, and it meant a serious decline in demand. An indication of the oversupply that existed was that Union Sulphur and Freeport Sulphur Company together had inventories equivalent to five times the amount of sulphur sold in many years before 1916.

Texas Gulf took the offensive. It built its own huge stockpiles. It developed new markets by converting sulphuric acid manufacturers from pyrites to sulphides and it promoted the use of sulphur in fertilizers. In 1921, Texas Gulf produced one million tons of sulphur for the first time; it also embarked on a program of acquiring more sulphur properties, and its shares were listed on the New York Stock Exchange, an event shortly followed by the payment of its first dividend.

The big three of the sulphur industry – Union, Freeport, and Texas Gulf – were all having difficulties in maintaining reserves. Union's original mine at Calcasieu Parrish in Louisiana was exhausted. Freeport developed some modest new reserves.

Despite the near-depletion of Big Hill dome, Texas Gulf became the world's biggest sulphur producer.

At the time, the company's geological department comprised one man, an engineer named Albert Wolf. Wolf became excited about the discovery of a new salt dome, later named Boling, where mineral leases were largely owned by a subsidiary of the Gulf Oil Corporation. In Wolf's words, it was "the most promising spot I had seen in my exploration of the Gulf Coast." Texas Gulf began to acquire the sulphur fee to these lands, and in the summer of 1927 made an agreement to buy the sulphur rights belonging to the Gulf Oil subsidiary in return for $3 million plus one-half of the net profit after Texas Gulf had recovered its development costs.

Texas Gulf began construction of a new company town, Newgulf (the first town, at the Big Hill dome, had been called Gulf). An indication of its size is given in an official company account.

> Included in the townsite were two dry goods stores, two pharmacies, a barber shop, a tailor and cleaning shop, three garages, a movie theater, a hospital, school, library, and a nine-hole golf course and clubhouse.

The plant was even more impressive at Boling dome, and it was due largely to Aldridge's engineering genius. In terms of efficiency and size, it far surpassed any other sulphur facility in the world. Production began at Boling dome on March 20, 1929.

The depression naturally slashed world sulphur consumption. When Texas Gulf's sales fell by 50% between 1929 and 1932, the Big Hill dome operation was shut down. Another more immediate consequence of the depression was that Texas Gulf was able to buy, for 1,300,000 newly issued treasury shares, the 50% share of profits that had earlier been contracted to Gulf Oil Corporation. The result of this 1934 transaction was that Gulf Oil Corporation now owned almost 35% of Texas Gulf Sulphur Company.

With an upturn in sulphur demand, Texas Gulf went about exploration. In 1936 the company optioned a property on the Ecstall River in British Columbia, the first venture for Texas Gulf in Canada. Other geologists ranged as far as Iraq and Iran in the search for sulphur. Always, under the direction of President Aldridge, the objective was sulphur to the exclusion of other minerals. Management remained traditional: It paid generous dividends, and the rest largely went into retained earnings.

The Second World War did not bring special prosperity to Texas Gulf, and in some ways the early years of the 1940s were spotted with disappointments. The company was anxious to bring a new mine, Moss Bluff, into production, but government controls and scarcity of equipment brought postponement of production plans. Towards the end of the war, the War Production Board, having decided that sulphur needs were not as critical as had been thought, imposed further restrictions.

Texas Gulf meanwhile turned to Mexico as a source of elemental sulphur. The company also helped to develop a means of purifying sour gas which had been found in quantity in southwestern Arkansas. The technique – desulphurization – was later put to good use when Texas Gulf built a $4 million sulphur recovery plant at the Worland gas field in Wyoming's Big Horn Basin. The Company was the first to produce sulphur from sour gas, and the technique later made Texas Gulf turn a serious eye toward Canada.

Within reasoned limits, sulphur consumption can be predicted into the future. Production trends are much more volatile: As the intense demand from the Korean War came to an end, new world supplies came on the market. The world had too much sulphur by 1952, and the oversupply was to persist for 10 years. Texas Gulf, with its sour gas process and its new development in Mexico, had contributed in a major way to the problem that plagued the industry.

Under the guidance of President Aldridge, Texas Gulf had survived well in an industry whose markets promised a traditional growth of only 4% per year. Aldridge was 83 when he resigned the presidency in 1951, but he stayed for another six years as chairman and his influence continued. His successor was Fred M. Nelson, who could hardly argue with the system when Texas Gulf's profits reached a record $32,356,000 or $3.23 per share in 1955 on sales of $93,589,000.

Not many companies, no matter what their business, can boast a ratio of profit to sales of one to three. When it came to the sulphur business, Texas Gulf was well and conservatively managed. It was a matter of pride that the company had no debt and had not felt the need to borrow for many years. Nelson put into force some modest exploration programs, but the defined object was never the discovery and development of other mineral reserves. Despite itself, Texas Gulf turned out some oil. But where oil lands were acquired, it was done under programs to buy or to protect sulphur deposits. When Texas Gulf chose to pump oil from the ground, it was usually to fuel its own power plants.

In many respects 1957 was the turning point for Texas Gulf. The world-wide recession reduced demand for sulphur, and production of Frasch sulphur declined by 12% in the United States. At the same time an increase in world production helped to cause a price decline from $26.50 to $23.50 per ton.

Shareholders were assured that Texas Gulf could still compete at lower prices and turn a profit, although it was superfluous to add that the rate of profit would be reduced. Notwithstanding, inventories of sulphur had grown to three million tons, more than half of all the sulphur consumed in the United States during the preceding year. This grim situation was reflected in Texas Gulf's financial statements. Sales declined to $66,883,847 from $88,573,412 the year before. Net profit fell even more precipitously, to $17,557,369 or $1.75 per share from $28,135,880 or $2.81 per share. In the fourth quarter, the dividend was cut from 50¢ to 25¢ so that the annual payout to shareholders could come entirely from earnings. It meant that exactly $22,369 was left over for retained earnings.

Moreover, the company was having trouble with its new venture in Mexico, a country which in 1957 had accounted for 15% of North America's total production. President Nelson had been offered but had rejected the opportunity to buy a Mexican property from Pan American Sulphur Co. Pan Am developed the property itself, and with an alumnus of Texas Gulf prominent among its managers, began to steal a big portion of the market. Later Texas Gulf tried to retaliate by cutting its own prices by $3 per ton, but this strategy failed and profits declined further.

There also was this notation in the 1957 Texas Gulf annual report:

> Thorough exploratory drilling of sulphur leases on salt domes off the Texas Gulf coast, although disclosing the presence of some sulphur, failed to prove any commercial deposits. In September, the company ceased these drilling operations and surrendered the leases to the state [of Texas].

Many years later, Texas Gulf Director Francis Coates was to relate how serious this disappointment had been. In his illustration, he attempted to draw an analogy to the results that might have followed the drilling of the first hole at Kidd Creek:

> . . . the one that sticks in my mind was 1955. Texas Gulf and Gulf Oil Corporation had done some geophysical work in that part of the Gulf of Mexico where the

minerals belong to Texas. Based on that geophysical work, they had bought sulphur leases for which they paid $7,100,000, and these bids were public, and the public knew it. They then drilled the salt dome. They could tell by geophysics that the dome was there and that it had caprock. They couldn't tell whether there was in that dome sulphur in commercial quantities. They core-drilled it. The first two or three cores looked beautiful, then they pinched out. There wasn't enough sulphur. There may have been two or three million tons of sulphur, but there wasn't enough to justify the expensive installation that it takes to produce sulphur commercially out in the Gulf of Mexico.

If 1957 showed that sulphur alone was an unsteady prop for Texas Gulf, it also brought signs that the nature of the company's management was about to change.

Three directors who had spent a total of 104 years on the board of Texas Gulf did not seek re-election. One of those was Walter H. Aldridge, president for 35 years and chairman for six, the man who symbolized the company's devotion to sulphur. Fred Nelson moved from the presidency to the board chairmanship, and a young petroleum engineer (at 47, young by Texas Gulf standards) became president.

Claude Odell Stephens had graduated from Louisiana State University in 1932 and began work with Texas Gulf as an $80-a-month driller's helper at Boling dome. He became a field engineer in 1938, and after advancing to major in the United States Army during the war, returned to Texas Gulf and later became manager of the company's Wyoming plant, which as pioneering the extraction of sulphur from sour gas.

By 1952 he was a vice-president and four years later a member of the board. It was TGS Director Thomas Lamont who was largely responsible for Stephens' appointment as president. Lamont later said of Stephens, "He was imaginative, able, he would come up [sic] to the company, he knew all the aspects of the company's business, he was alert, he was aggressive, and he was a man of unquestioned integrity."

At the end of 1957, Texas Gulf itself was the picture of integrity in a fiscal sense. It had a working capital of more than $66 million and still no debt. Its current assets were twelve times its incredibly modest current liabilities of $6,165,534. Although the annual report referred to the search for recovering sulphur and associated metals from sulphide ore deposits "such as those owned in Canada," there was no specific reference to the company's Canadian Shield exploration program, which had begun that year.

Chapter Six

TEXAS GULF COMES TO CANADA

The turning point in the fortunes of Texas Gulf Sulphur was 1957. Claude Stephens, the new president, was not to become chief executive officer for another four years; still his consciousness of the company's over-reliance on the vacillations of the sulphur market was felt throughout the organizations. "We're not ultraconservative all the way through," he said at the time.

An important development that year was the appointment of Charles Fogarty as vice-president and manager of exploration. Fogarty was not yet 40; although his experience from the time he joined Texas Gulf in 1952 had dealt mainly with exploration for sulphur, he was mindful of other opportunities that lay before the company. He was brilliant and in fact he had won his doctorate in geology at the Colorado School of Mines in record time.

Texas Gulf went on a worldwide hunt for sulphides, and now it didn't matter that the sulphides might be associated with metals rather than as a source of sulphur. One memorandum that had been written by an employee in the company's exploration department just prior to that time included this startling comment: "I fear that lead, zinc, copper is not a product we want, no matter how big the deposit." That attitude was soon to change.

Texas Gulf had owned a low-grade ore deposit in the Ecstall region of British Columbia since the 1930s, but the company's interest in Canada didn't intensify until the Canadian Shield program was begun in 1957. At first the program took the form of studies of existing mines and a great deal of contemplation. Walter Holyk, the young Canadian geologist, was developing his own theories about the types of rock formations that lent themselves to mineral concentrations in the Shield, and another Texas Gulf geologist, Leo Miller, was assigned to conduct a coast-to-coast analysis of the geology of known mines.

Miller spent parts of 1957, 1958, 1959, and 1960 on this project and chose nine comparatively virgin areas which he thought would be worthy of examination. These areas were small in relation to the total breadth of the 1,864,000-square-mile shield, but in practical terms they were large enough – as much as 50 miles square – that finding a mine might have been compared to finding a needle in a haystack. One of these areas he named the Alexo Basin, 40 miles long and 12 miles wide, which embraced the site of the eventual Kidd Creek discovery.

Texas Gulf's first intensive exploration was on a property in New Brunswick, where drilling almost produced a productive mine. In 1962 the company began drilling on the northern tip of Baffin Island above Hudson Bay. The lead-zinc-silver ore showed good values, but because of the remoteness of the deposit, the Baffin Island property did not immediately become a mine.

After the discovery of the Kidd Creek mine in 1963, and when Texas Gulf began to be quizzed about the significance of Kidd Creek to its overall operations, the company tried hard to emphasize the importance of the New Brunswick and Baffin Island properties. "Even in late 1963," Stephens said some time later, these properties were considered by the company to be "mineable orebodies." The contention of the Securities and Exchange Commission, on the other hand, was that the Kidd Creek mine alone opened up a "whole new horizon" of opportunity for the company, and itself was the reason Texas Gulf established a new metals division.

Certainly the company's predominant interest in Canada showed a radical change after the Kidd Creek discovery. In early 1963 the annual return of the company as submitted to the government of the Province of Ontario showed its main business in Canada to be the production and marketing of sulphur through its sour gas properties in Alberta.

In 1964 Texas Gulf applied to the Government of Ontario to have its objectives amended to allow it to use as much as $50 million to "process, combine, change the form of, manufacture and perform all other acts necessary or desirable to convert . . . minerals and metals. . . ."

Texas Gulf, in Canada at least, was no longer a sulphur company.

Chapter Seven

THE HENDRIE PROPERTY

The person who stands to derive by far the greatest financial benefit from the discovery of the Kidd Creek Mine is a retired businessman living in Hamilton, Ontario, the sooty capital of Canada's steelmaking industry, 40 miles from Toronto on the western point of Lake Ontario. William Alexander Turner Gilmour never owned a share of stock in Texas Gulf Sulphur Company; until the early 1960s he had never even heard of the company. Suddenly he became entitled to 10% of the net profit from what may be the greatest base metals mine in the world.

It wasn't until after the turn of this century that mining men began to look to the Canadian Shield as an attractive region to explore for valuable metals. Gold discoveries had been made in southeastern Ontario and in the Lake of the Woods area near the Ontario-Manitoba border, but there was little profitable production. Some iron ore was found, but nothing to compare to the great iron ranges in Wisconsin, Minnesota, and Michigan along the south shore of Lake Superior. In the early 1880s, during construction of the Canadian Pacific Railway, sulphide deposits containing nickel and copper were found at Sudbury, but it was 30 or 40 years before metallurgical problems were solved and markets developed which allowed the Sudbury basin to become one of the greatest mining centers of the world.

The Ontario government was ignorant of the mineral riches in and around the Porcupine area, but there was timber and pulpwood there, and some of the land was arable, despite the forbidding winters. In 1903 the government undertook to finance the Temiskaming and Northern Ontario Railway to open up the land around what is now Timmins.

Northern Ontario was then, and remains to this day, set apart from the southern part of the province by economics as well as by geography. The government was anxious to open up the land for agricultural purposes and attempted to induce colonization by making generous land grants to veterans of the Boer War and the Fenian Raids. The legislation was provided under "An Act to Provide for the Appropriation of Certain Lands for the Volunteers Who Served in South Africa and the Volunteer Militia Who Served on the Frontier in 1866." The land grants included the surface rights, timber rights, and mineral rights.

One of the grantees was Murray Hendrie, a 32-year-old veteran of the Boer War. Hendrie was deeded a parcel of 159 acres more or less, known as the north half of Lot No. 3 in the Fifth Concession of Kidd Township.

Hendrie hardly needed this charity: He came from one of the wealthiest families, and certainly the most prominent family in Hamilton, Ontario. His father, William Hendrie, was a self-made man: contractor, railway cartage agent, manufacturer. He also had a famous horse-breeding establishment. The family residence, called the Holmstead, covered a large city block and was a stopping place for two future kings of England, George V and George VI. An indication of the Hendrie family's substance was that William provided in his will that his wife should get an income sufficient "for the maintenance of the affairs of the Holmstead, which will cover all expenses incurred there, including servants, gardeners, coachmen, horses and all costs and expenses necessary to maintain the Holmstead. . . ."

There is no evidence to suggest that Murray Hendrie, one of William's 11 children, paid particular attention to the land granted him by the government. On the contrary, it seems he altogether forgot about it.

For some reason Murray chose not to enter the family business but instead moved to High River, north of Calgary, Alberta, and engaged in the business of ranching. It is likely that his love for horses helped to set him on this course; the Hendries were horsey people, and photographs remain in the family archives showing Murray in the saddle.

Murray returned to Hamilton briefly at Christmastime 1910, and took as his wife a 33-year-old widow, Agnes Rachel Gilmour. The former Mrs. Gilmour (who lived to witness the Kidd Creek discovery) had a seven-year-old son, William Alexander Turner Gilmour. Within a week of his marriage, on January 4, 1911, Murray Hendrie made his last will and testament.

In his will, Murray Hendrie either forgot or didn't bother to mention the remote piece of forlorn property that had been granted to him by the government of Ontario. It was no wonder; when he died in an accident on October 17, 1914, his assets were computed to be worth $230,455.19. There can be no doubt that Murray neglected to tell his wife about the 159-acre plot in Kidd Township; and it's just as likely that Murray's two brothers, who were executors of his estate, had no knowledge of the land.

In any event, the first recorded instance that the Murray Hendrie estate became aware of the Kidd property was in February 1926 – 12 years after his death. By this time the Royal Trust Company, one of Canada's largest financial institutions, had become executor of the estate. Out of the blue came a letter from a Mulholland and Company, inquiring of the Royal Trust what price the Hendrie estate would take for the north half of Lot 3, Concession V, Kidd Township.

Mulholland and Company followed up a month later with a further letter stating it was prepared to pay between $150 and $200 for the property.

During the next few years there was a regular incidence of correspondence between the Royal Trust Company and prospective bidders for the Kidd property. A Mohawk Timber and Land Company informed the executors of the Hendrie estate that lots in Kidd Township were bringing between $200 and $300. In the light of that advice, Royal Trust asked Mulholland and Company to make a firm bid, and Mulholland subsequently offered $300 cash. It was a generous offer (and would have seemed more so in the depression years), but Royal Trust was cautioned by a member of the Hendrie family that "he did not think it necessary to sell the Kidd property."

Some productive farms grew up along the route of what was the Temiskaming and Northern Ontario Railway, but generally only where nearby mining communities provided a market for agricultural produce.

Most of the land grant properties were never used for agricultural purposes, and in 1963 some were still held by heirs and descendants of the original grantees. Most of the properties had been acquired at low prices, especially during the depression years, by lumber and pulpwood companies. Whatever advances may have been made to Royal Trust in reference to the Hendrie estate during the 1930s were apparently repelled.

In 1939 the Royal Trust Company decided to take the initiative. It inquired of the Ontario Department of Lands and Forests regarding the value of the Kidd property, and was referred to Abitibi Power and Paper Company, one of eastern Canada's biggest pulp producers. Royal Trust wrote Abitibi offering to sell the land but there is no record of any reply from Abitibi. Royal Trust then attempted to sell the Hendrie property to an Arrow Land and Logging Company, but Arrow said it was not interested.

On one occasion in 1944, Royal Trust was advised by "one J. J. McKay of Timmins" that "there would not be any mineral values but there might be considerable timber value." At the end of the war, Royal Trust was given an estimate that the value of the wood on the Hendrie property, at prevailing prices of $1.60 per cord, was $3,000.

T. S. Woollings and Company, the pulpwood subsidiary of Curtis Publishing Company, made a cash offer of $2,000 for the Hendrie property in 1951. Woollings might have been successful had not a Timmins forest engineer submitted a counter-offer of $2,500 for the timber rights alone. There is not as much discrepancy as there seems between the Woollings offer and the successful bid; after all, the land was thought to offer little or nothing of value other than the timber rights. Sale of the timber concession tied up the rights to the Hendrie property for ten years, until July, 1961.

It was two years earlier than that expiry date that Walter Holyk, Ken Darke, and Hugh Clayton had begun to conduct aerial geophysical surveys over what finally amounted to more than 15,000 miles of the Canadian Shield. In all, the Texas Gulf airborne crew went over the Kidd 55 area, including the Hendrie property, five times; three times in 1959 and twice in 1960. In each instance they detected an anomaly, a variation of the physical properties of the earth.

The aerial surveys found several hundred anomalies north and west of Timmins, but the one centered on the Hendrie property, later designated Kidd 55, gave one of the strongest reactions on the electromagnetic recorder. The possible significance of the anomaly is verified by the fact that Texas Gulf almost immediately began what turned out to be protracted negotiations with the owners of the Hendrie property and the lands surrounding the anomaly.

Also in the summer of 1959, Texas Gulf made a change in policy which may have been prompted by its desire to acquire the Kidd properties. The company adopted the practice, generally employed in the mining industry, of giving the property owner a 10% interest in the profits from any mine that might be discovered under their land. Eventually the negotiations with the four owners of the land beneath which the anomaly lay were carried on with this new policy in mind.

The four owners of the equal-sized lots were the Hendrie estate, Curtis Publishing's subsidiary, the T. S. Woollings Company, and two private estates identified as "J. F. Elliott" and "J. H. Roberts."

Leo Miller, a Texas Gulf geologist, set out the ownership of these properties in a memorandum dated April 2, 1959. He went on to say, "From our experience with the airborne equipment to date . . . and from the geological data available, I believe that this anomaly is due to massive sulphides (75 per cent at least). . . ." Massive sulphides occur where the concentration of the sulphides is such that they are together, thereby permitting a flow of electricity from a geophysical survey.

The first contact that Texas Gulf made with the Royal Trust Company was on January 24, 1961, when Walter Holyk, the company's chief geologist, telephoned Royal Trust's office in Toronto. For months thereafter there was a series of negotiations which from Texas Gulf's point of view were highly delicate. Nothing could better illustrate this than a letter written to the trust company on November 3, 1961, a masterpiece of "cool":

Dear Sirs: *Re: Murray Hendrie Estate.*

It has come to our attention by a telephone conversation with your Mr. A. E. Love that the Royal Trust Company is executor of the Murray Hendrie Estate. We are interested in arranging an option to cover mineral and surface rights owned by the estate in the N.1/2, Lot 3, Concession V, Kidd Township, Ontario.

The mining exploration department of Texas Gulf Sulphur Company has performed extensive work in the Timmins area on Crown lands. To complete our assessment of the area we are considering possible groundwork on lands held by private individuals or companies.

The usual mining option concerning a situation of this type whereby a mining company bears all costs of exploration, provides a small interest in any eventual discovery made on the title holder's land during the option period.

If a general proposal of this nature is attractive to you we would like to discuss details and if possible come to an equitable agreement.

Yours very truly,
Texas Gulf Sulphur Company
D. A. Lowrie.

DAL/mch

Several months later Texas Gulf submitted a proposed option agreement. Royal Trust suggested some changes, which were agreed to in June, 1962. A revised draft of the option agreement was sent to Royal Trust.

There was a delay of another six months, and Texas Gulf became increasingly fidgety. Holyk wrote to Royal Trust in February, 1963, saying he would be pleased to hear some decision about the option agreement. Yes, replied the trust company, the agreement was being considered, and it was hoped that a decision could be made within two weeks.

On May 24, 1963, Holyk finally got word; Royal Trust was prepared to enter into the option agreement provided some additional changes were made. If Texas Gulf were agreeable, would it kindly forward the final draft of the option agreement with a cheque in the amount of $500? It took Texas Gulf less than 10 days to consider the revisions, accept the agreement, and dispatch the cheque to Royal Trust. The agreement was executed June 6, 1963.

The agreement entitled Texas Gulf to explore the Hendrie property for up to two years. During this period, Texas Gulf could, by the payment of $18,000 U.S., acquire mining rights to the property. If the company were to exercise the option, and if it were to discover a commercial deposit of ore, then the Hendrie estate was to have a 10% participation in any profits.

Meanwhile, Texas Gulf was continuing its efforts to obtain mining rights to the three adjoining properties. In October, 1961, Holyk instructed David Lowrie of the company's exploration department to press negotiations with T. S. Woollings Company for rights to the 160-acre lot which lay diagonally southwest of the Hendrie property. A month later Ken Darke visited the Woollings office in South Porcupine, which is all but a suburb of Timmins. James Reid, Woollings' general manager, was "most receptive to the idea of an option agreement between the two companies."

Darke reported back to New York, and Texas Gulf's Lowrie

wrote to Reid in November, 1961, presenting a general and tentative proposal for an option agreement. It was broad in scope and very complicated, calling for Texas Gulf to acquire the rights to Woollings' lands in six townships. Woollings responded by putting the squeeze on Texas Gulf; A. L. Bennett, Woollings' president, visited Texas Gulf's Toronto office, expressed interest in some sort of arrangement, but mentioned that another company was also interested in the lands.

Judging by the ensuing events, Woollings was even more willing to sell its properties than Texas Gulf was anxious to buy them. Woollings made the next move, with a letter some months later inquiring whether Texas Gulf was still interested in a deal and not neglecting to mention the anonymous company which also was supposedly on the sidelines. In July, 1962, Holyk replied by saying that Texas Gulf had embraced a new policy; Holyk proposed that Texas Gulf option from Woollings several specific lots at a fixed price per acre, with a 10% interest to be retained by Woollings.

An option agreement between Texas Gulf and Woollings was executed on February 4, 1964, almost three months after the Kidd Creek discovery hole. It was for three years, for the consideration of $11,588.50.

South of the Hendrie property was the J. H. Roberts Estate property. Texas Gulf began negotiations on July 27, 1959, when Holyk called the solicitor for the estate. Holyk wrote to the lawyer the same day, suggesting a two-year option for $25,000; $200 upon execution of the agreement, $300 upon renewal of the option for the second year, and the balance if the option were exercised. The Texas Gulf exploration department made many further attempts, all abortive, to acquire the Roberts property through its lawyer. However, Texas Gulf did finally negotiate an agreement with beneficiaries of the Roberts estate.

There is little recorded evidence about Texas Gulf's attempts to acquire the J. F. Elliott estate, the land directly to the east of the Hendrie property. This property was acquired in December 1963, but it was of little consequence. No part of the orebody lies beneath the former Elliott property.

In total, Texas Gulf acquired the three properties adjoining the Hendrie estate property for an outlay of $59,500.

It was alleged in a later lawsuit that the time lapse of five years in Texas Gulf's acquisition of these properties meant that its interest in the Kidd 55 anomaly was exhausted. It was an argument which had little impact on the judge, who commented:

> . . . for obviously Texas Gulf could not push the negotiations too hard without causing the prospective vendors to suspect that a discovery had been made, in which event either purchases would have become impossible or prices grossly inflated. Under the circumstances, I believe that Texas Gulf did what any prudent mining company would have done to acquire property in which it knew a very promising anomaly lay.

This judicial comment was not meant to reflect on yet another legal action taken against Texas Gulf over its acquisition of the Hendrie property.

The publicity generated by Texas Gulf's discovery of the Kidd Creek mine brought to light certain circumstances which the Royal Trust Company, for one, felt had a bearing on previous agreements. Royal Trust, acting for the Hendrie estate, charged that the $18,000 option agreement whereby Texas Gulf had acquired the major portion of the Kidd Creek orebody had been entered into as a result of misrepresentation. It sought to recover the orebody for the Hendrie estate.

Royal Trust said that the statement, ". . . we are considering possible groundwork on lands held by private individuals or companies," constituted a representation by Texas Gulf that it had yet done no groundwork on the Hendrie property. Royal Trust said this and other alleged misrepresentations indicated that Texas Gulf intended to mislead.

Texas Gulf's response was an admission that two of its employees on one occasion had been on the Hendrie property, in an attempt to locate more precisely the anomaly which had been detected from aerial surveys.

> The purpose thereof was to endeavour to determine the location of the anomaly with respect to property boundaries so as to learn with what owners negotiation for options or other rights would be appropriate.
>
> Such employees did not damage or disturb the Hendrie property in any way. Except as herein stated, the defendant [Texas Gulf] made no geological or geophysical tests or observations of the Hendrie property at any time prior to June 6, 1963 [the date of the option agreement].

(It is of interest that Royal Trust is sufficiently optimistic about their chances that every month they return the cheque for several hundred thousand dollars that Texas Gulf Sulphur mails to them as their 10% share of the profits.)

Texas Gulf – obviously having in mind its pending court battle with an agency of the United States Government – further denied that rock outcrops indicating mineralization combined with the evidence of a present anomaly "provided an unusually promising indication of economic mineralization on the Hendrie property."

Agnes Rachel Gilmour Hendrie, Murray Hendrie's widow, witnessed these arguments before she died in her 92nd year on February 26, 1968. At the time of her death the estate contained investments and other assets worth more than $300,000 – plus the 10% interest in profits from the Kidd Creek mine. Without the latter, her son William Alexander Turner Gilmour might have gone unchallenged as the sole heir to the estate. With the mine interest, and perhaps because of it, the disposition of the estate was challenged by approximately 100 of the descendants of Murray Hendrie's brothers and sisters.

Murray's will had provided that after the death of his wife his estate was to be divided "among all my children." He further took the precaution that in the event "of there being no children of mine living at the death of my said wife . . ." then the estate was to be divided among his brothers and sisters or their descendants.

The will raised the question of whether William Alexander Turner Gilmour, the only son of Agnes Hendrie by her first marriage, was a "child" of Murray Hendrie. Courts have been asked to interpret words such as these in countless cases where the intent of a will might be altered by circumstances following the testator's death. Generally the courts have treated each case on its own merits. In the Hendrie case an Ontario Supreme Court justice decided that "child" was not a word restricted to mean an infant born of a man and woman. The judge held that,

> . . . although he (Murray Hendrie) may well have contemplated fathering children, of whom his wife would be the mother . . . he had dependent upon him for his daily support, guidance and direction a little boy of very tender years whose natural father had died months before he was born. He brought this child into his very family, – his household.

William Alexander Turner Gilmour was therefore judged to qualify for a one-tenth share of the profits that ensue from one of the richest base metals discoveries in the world – his share is estimated to be worth over $100 million.

Chapter Eight

THE MAN WHO MADE 100 MILLION DOLLARS

It was January 21, 1969, and all the newspapers carried the story. The Ontario Supreme Court had named William A. T. Gilmour of Hamilton sole beneficiary of the estate of his stepfather, Murray Hendrie. What it really meant was that Gilmour and his heirs would get 10% of the gross profits of the Texas Gulf Sulphur Co.'s Kidd Township production. It would mean for Gilmour an annual income of up to $10 million. The 100 descendants of Murray Hendrie's ten brothers and sisters would get nothing.

The story didn't get the play you might expect of a court decision that makes a man a multi-millionaire overnight, possibly because everyone expected that the other relatives would appeal, as has happened.

Bill Gilmour was happy that day – not so much over the court decision, but because it drew so little public attention. If there is one thing Bill Gilmour dislikes, it is personal publicity of any kind. The story in Toronto's *Globe and Mail* the next day contained only a very brief statement by Gilmour:

I'm very pleased, of course, but I understand some of the others who lost are planning an appeal against the judgment.

I was surprised by the outcome because it was a complicated matter, and I wasn't at all sure the decision would be in my favour.

He agreed that the 10% of the profit of the Timmins mine would be a very substantial sum, but added, "I'll get what's left after the government gets its share."

The city editor of the *Hamilton Spectator*, the only paper in Gilmour's home city, assigned reporter Jerry Rogers to interview Gilmour, now suddenly one of Canada's richest men, if not the richest. (If the Royal Trust wins the suit they have brought on behalf of the Murray Hendrie estate against Texas Gulf Sulphur, Bill Gilmour may end up by owning the entire two billion dollar orebody and will be not only the richest man in Canada but one of the richest in the world.)

Gilmour refused to discuss the matter. His brief statement to the *Globe and Mail* was repeated word-for-word in the *Spectator* story, but because Thomas W. D. Farmer, the *Spectator*'s editor-in-chief, is one of Gilmour's closest associates, Mr. Gilmour did supply the *Spectator* with photographs of his mother and of Murray Hendrie. (When I subsequently asked Mr. Gilmour if I could have copies of those photographs for this book, he agreed to forward the photograph of Hendrie but said, "I don't really think I want a picture of my mother in a book.")

William Alexander Turner Gilmour is a tall, slender, good-looking man of 66 whose old-fashioned schoolboy haircut and neatly trimmed mustache make him look like a highly successful corporation lawyer – a great distortion of his real personality.

He is shy, quiet, soft spoken – not quite unapproachable, but a definite introvert whose nervousness is betrayed by a slight stutter in his speech. He lives with his wife, Margaret, and one of his two daughters in a big, lavishly furnished $65,000 French-Canadian style home on St. James Place in Hamilton, an exclusive court with just nine homes tucked under the mountain less than a dozen blocks from the city's busy downtown. His neighbours include an Anglican bishop, two doctors, two lawyers, a rich scrap metal dealer, and two wealthy widows, none of whom know anything about his personal life. William Gilmour is the opposite of the popular picture of a man newly come to great wealth.

Nothing he does attracts attention. He doesn't drive big expensive cars; his wife has a 1965 Chevrolet convertible and he drives a 1968 Rambler American. He is without doubt a member of Hamilton's Establishment, but only by virtue of his independent wealth and family connections.

Bill Gilmour was born in Hamilton in 1903, the son of Agnes Rachel Turner and William Alexander Gilmour, a young lawyer who died before he reached the age of 30. It was when he was seven that his mother married Murray Hendrie, a former Hamiltonian then cattle ranching at High River, Alberta. But Bill Gilmour's life on a ranch was short lived. His stepfather died after four years and he and his widowed mother returned to Hamilton.

He spent his school days out West at Western Canada College, a private boys' school in Calgary, and when he arrived back in Hamilton, was sent to Appleby College, a private school at Oakville. After Appleby he went on to McGill University in Montreal, graduating in 1925 in mechanical engineering and a year later in electrical engineering with the British Association medal. He described himself as an "average" student. "I was never outstanding," he says. He played a bit of hockey and cricket but only because it was expected of every student.

Once through university, he went to work at the Smart-Turner Machine Company Ltd. in Hamilton. It was a small firm founded in 1902 by his uncle, John A. Turner, and W. G. Smart. The firm, whose office was located in an old stone building at 191 Barton Street East beside the century-old Barton Street Jail, manufactured barrels and industrial pumps that were used to move every kind of liquid imaginable – from sewage to soup. During the war years the company was kept extremely busy by the navy making pumps and barrels, which were used to cellularize the holds of merchant ships to keep them afloat in case of torpedoing.

When Bill Gilmour joined the company in 1926, he went to work in the engineering department. It was a small company with about 90 employees who all worked closely together.

John Strachan, a former Hamilton Tiger-Cat football player who now sells real estate in Hamilton worked as a machinist at the Smart-Turner plant 15 years ago. He remembers Bill Gilmour as:

> . . . a quiet, very friendly person, but one who kept to himself and didn't mix much with other employees.
>
> He had a lot of respect because he carried respect for others. I never heard him ever say anything derogatory about anyone. He never pushed his weight around, minded his own business and never got into any squabbles.
>
> Bill always contributed to anything the employees wanted – I remember he contributed towards our ball team. He was just a plain nice guy.

No one can recall Bill Gilmour's being an aggressive

worker with tremendous ambition to get to the top; his succession, however, was taken for granted. When John Turner died in 1954, Bill Gilmour took over as president.

In 1959, just five years later, he sold out to American interests. Smart-Turner was taken over by the Hamilton-Thomas Corporation, whose subsidiary, the C. W. Wheeler Manufacturing Company of Philadelphia, manufactured a line of pumps similar to those made by Smart-Turner.

The barrel machinery business was sold and expensive equipment was installed at Smart-Turner to make Hamilton-Thomas heat-transfer products for the Canadian market. But then acquisition of the Hamilton-Thomas interests by the Baldwin-Lima-Hamilton Corporation of Philadelphia resulted in a change of manufacturing plans. The new owners, who specialized in heavy machinery, decided to withdraw from the Canadian market. In order to protect family interests in the preferred shares and bonds, Bill Gilmour bought out the common shares in April of 1962 and became president of the company once again.

By then the work force had dwindled to 50. The company had fallen into the red to the extent of $125,000, according to Mr. Gilmour, but two years later, when he sold out again – this time to a Canadian – he had not only recouped the loss but had the firm making a healthy profit.

Bill Gilmour doesn't seem to be the kind of man who was ever really interested in carving a big business career for himself. He certainly had the money and the opportunity; if he lacked anything it was ambition. He has always stayed close to his family and home. Married in 1930 to a girl from an equally well-to-do family from Montreal, Bill Gilmour moved into his St. James Place home two years later and has been there ever since. Mrs. (Margaret) Gilmour leads an active, but unpublicized life, and is involved with service work.

William Gilmour has two daughters who will inherit his

fortune. The younger, Mary, now about 30, is still single and works as a nursing supervisor in the emergency ward at the Hamilton General Hospital. His elder daughter is now Nancy Keen, the mother of three children married to a business consultant and lives in Magog, Quebec.

If Bill Gilmour has any kind of a reputation it is confined to his interests as a naturalist. His deep interest in nature, birds, and photography has colored his quiet life. He is secretary of the Hamilton Naturalist Club and a director of the Color Photography Club of Hamilton. He owns several hundred dollars worth of photographic equipment and spends hours watching birds nest, waiting to photograph the young being born. He has written several articles for the Hamilton Naturalist's Club monthly bulletin and is active in church work. He has been treasurer of MacNab Street Presbyterian Church, where his grandfather was chairman of the board, for the past three years and has served in other capacities in other years.

His connections with the Establishment in Hamilton have been maintained through membership in the Hamilton Club – a private men's club at which he frequently eats lunch – and the exclusive 150-member Tamahaac Club at Ancaster, of which he is a governor. Bill Gilmour has never travelled extensively. His summers are spent between the summer home that belonged to his wife's family on the St. Lawrence River at Rivière-du-Loup, Quebec, and a private summer home on an island in Lake Muskoka, Ontario, formerly owned by his uncle.

Few people who know Bill Gilmour know him intimately. Artist Frank Panabaker of Ancaster has known the Gilmour family for 25 years. In fact, several of his paintings – landscapes – hang in the dining room of the Gilmour home. "Bill is an extraordinary nice fellow. He is not favorably impressed by people who keep referring to his wealth," says Panabaker,

And he adds, "No, I can't honestly tell you who his closest friends are."

Mrs. W. R. Shivas of Dundas, an ardent naturalist who has known Bill Gilmour all her life, said, "Indeed, you would never know he has wealth. He is certainly not ostentatious in any way. I don't think Bill has ever been anything different."

Dr. John Johnston, minister at MacNab Street Presbyterian Church, says Bill Gilmour is "quiet, unassuming but delightful, efficient, and perceptive. No, his wealth certainly doesn't show."

William Gilmour is the individual who has gained more financially than any other human being from the Texas Gulf discovery. It is doubtful that his added wealth will make one iota of difference to his life.

Chapter Nine

KEN DARKE MAKES HIS PRIVATE FORTUNE

The April 16 announcement of Texas Gulf's discovery caused the 29,985 population of Timmins to swell by more than 5,000 as fortune hunters descended on the town to jockey for a piece of the land near Kidd Township. There was no room at the 25 small hotels and motels, and the overflow of visitors littered the lobbies at night. The caravan that made its way into Timmins included cars with license plates from as far away as Florida and California. Snowshoes, at $40 a pair, were the scarcest commodity, and rope, tents, and sleeping bags were almost as hard to come by. The Fountain Court Bar in the Empire Hotel, the bona-fide clearing house for rumors, reports, and all manner of gossip, was fully occupied from midafternoon until after the one a.m. closing time. Texas Gulf was not the focus of discussion, as its shares had already risen from $15 to $44 by the end of the month. Rather, it was the penny mining companies, whose low-priced shares had higher leverage, promised much faster gains, and of course carried an infinitely higher risk.

There were soon more than 100 companies with property in a 20-mile radius sweeping north, east, and west from Timmins. In one of the more bizarre incidents, Royal Canadian Mounted Police were required to maintain surveillance at the Timmins airport so that stakers would not plant their posts near the runways. Despite this vigilance, a staking group laid their claim to some airport land and sold the rights to the International Nickel Company of Canada. When the mining recorder refused to accept the claim papers, Inco appealed, unsuccessfully, to the Ontario Department of Mines.

The two brokerage firms in Timmins, whose offices were 35 yards apart on Pine Street, were doing a landslide business. A third firm, Draper Dobie and Company, one of Canada's biggest specialists in mining stocks, made plans to open a Timmins branch. At times it was impossible to squeeze into either of the existing offices in Timmins, and strollers along Pine Street were occasionally forced to step off the curb to continue on their way.

Mike Ayoub, a Timmins pioneer and by now the town's supermarket czar, replaced trading stamps with penny mining shares. A florist displayed this window sign: "Take home a dozen roses to help her get over the shock. P.S. – I wanna get rich, too." Mayor Leo Del Villano, a portly liquor salesman, appointed himself town greeter and announced to the stream of newspaper and magazine reporters who passed his door, "We're sitting on top of a jewelry store."

Maybe that was true, but even if it was, the public was looking in the wrong place. Most of the razzmatazz mining stocks that helped to churn trading volume to a record 28 million shares in one day on the Toronto Stock Exchange had acquired their mining claims from one source. Unknown to many of these companies, and certainly unknown to the public, much of this high-priced land had been previously inspected by Texas Gulf and judged worthless. How much would that knowledge have tempered the speculative fever that afflicted buyers of Timmins stocks?

Even in those frantic few weeks, Timmins was not the gaudy place that the mass media found it convenient to describe. In stories carried by mass circulation magazines, every prospector was grizzled and every matron was clinging hopefully to a fistful of mining shares. They said that Timmins was a frontier town, snowbound almost the year 'round and reeking with personalities out of Robert Service. It wasn't quite that way.

In the get-rich-quick atmosphere that had been created by the chroniclers of the Timmins boom, there was a sore need for a rags-to-riches hero. Such was Nedo Bragagnolo, and he made himself a willing ally to those who cultivated the myth. Bragagnolo had all the qualifications, not the least of which was that he was born of poor Italian immigrants. "We always had to hustle to make ends meet," he compliantly told reporters. But his newfound riches wouldn't change him – "I'll still wash my car and cut the grass."

Bragagnolo was 33 years old, thickset, and handsome, with a low forehead and black wavy hair. When he was 12, his father died of silicosis, a respiratory disease contracted from working underground in the mines. Young Nedo worked for a while as a surveyor in the mines, but he left to become an insurance salesman and later a real estate salesman.

"Nedo Bragagnolo is the boy wonder of the great Timmins copper boom. . . . He has parlayed $7,000 into possibly $2,000,000 . . ." was the beginning of one story in the *Toronto*

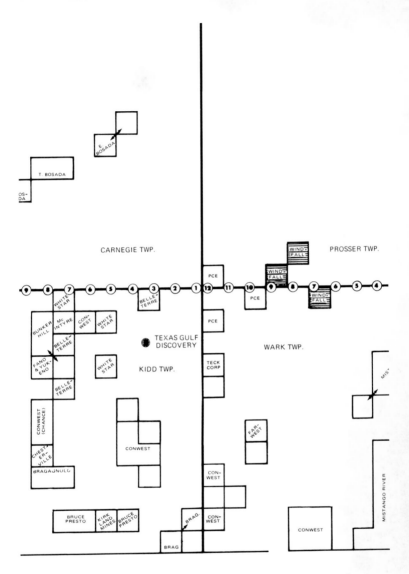

"Timmins staking spreads for miles in all directions as enthusiasm continues." The map of the discovery site published by the Northern Miner *on April 23, 1964.*

Ken Darke, geologist for Texas Gulf, made a fortune by selling claims surrounding the Texas Gulf discovery.

Downtown Timmins, Christmas 1964.

Dr. Walter Holyk, chief geologist of Texas Gulf, had the idea which led to the two-billion dollar ore discovery.

Site of the mine, November 1963.

Purchase Date	Purchaser	Shares Number	Price	Calls Number	Price

Hole K-55-1 Completed November 12, 1963

1963

Nov. 12	Fogarty	300	17¾-18		
15	Clayton	200	17¾		
15	Fogarty	700	17⅝-17⅞		
15	Mollison	100	17⅞		
19	Fogarty	500	18⅛		
26	Fogarty	200	17¾		
29	Holyk (Mrs.)	50	18		

Chemical Assays of Drill Core of K-55-1 Received December 9-13, 1963

Dec. 10	Holyk (Mrs.)	100	20⅜		
12	Holyk (or wife)			200	21
13	Mollison	100	21⅛		
30	Fogarty	200	22		
31	Fogarty	100	23¼		

1964

Jan. 6	Holyk (or wife)			100	23⅝
8	Murray			400	23¼
24	Holyk (or wife)			200	22¼-22⅜
Feb. 10	Fogarty	300	22⅛-22¼		
20	Darke	300	24⅛		
24	Clayton	400	23⅞		
24	Holyk (or wife)			200	24⅛
26	Holyk (or wife)			200	23⅜
26	Huntington	50	23¼		
27	Darke (Moran as nominee)			1000	22⅝-22¾
Mar. 2	Holyk (Mrs.)	200	22⅜		
3	Clayton	100	22¼		
16	Huntington			100	22⅜
16	Holyk (or wife)			300	23¼
17	Holyk (Mrs.)	100	23⅞		
23	Darke			1000	24¾
26	Clayton	200	25		

Purchase Date	Purchaser	Shares Number	Price	Calls Number	Price
Land Acquisition Completed March 27, 1964					
Mar. 30	Darke			1000	25½
30	Holyk (Mrs.)	100	25⅞		
Core Drilling of Kidd Segment Resumed March 31, 1964					
April 1	Clayton	60	26½		
1	Fogarty	400	26½		
2	Clayton	100	26⅞		
6	Fogarty	400	28⅛-28⅞		
8	Mollison (Mrs.)	100	28⅛		
First Press Release Issued April 12, 1964					
April 15	Clayton	200	29⅜		
16	Crawford (and wife)	600	30⅛-30¼		
Second Press Release Issued 10:00-10:10 or 10:15 a.m., April 16, 1964					
April 16	(app. 10:20 a.m.)				
	Coates (for family trusts)	2000	31-31⅝		

Neither Murray Hendrie nor his executor knew that he owned a two-billion-dollar orebody. His executor sold an option on it for $500.

Nedo Bragagnolo, left, made one million dollars in partnership with Ken Darke.

Karl Springer claimed his small company owned the rights to the Texas Gulf discovery.

George and Viola MacMillan were charged with fraud after the Windfall collapse, then acquitted.

Dr. Charles F. Fogarty, left, executive vice-president of Texas Gulf, was charged by the SEC *with using inside information for his personal advantage. R. H. Clayton, Texas Gulf geophysicist, was charged with using inside information before the public was informed.*

Richard Mollison, Texas Gulf's exploration manager, was charged by the SEC with using inside information for his personal advantage. His acquittal has been reversed and is now under review.

Claude Stephens, president of Texas Gulf Sulphur, was charged by the SEC with accepting options on TGS stock without disclosing material information about the Timmins drilling. His acquittal was reversed and is now under review.

The mine today.

Daily Star, Canada's largest newspaper, and it set the pattern for a repetition of the fascinating but untrue yarn about the wheeler-dealer who was the first outsider to divine that Texas Gulf had made an important strike.

Newsweek reported that Bragagnolo first became suspicious during the winter of 1963-4 after he noticed that ". . . a Texas Gulf helicopter was flying over the area every day." *True* magazine, in a breathless account, gave a more dramatic explanation: "On the rare instances of late where he had spotted the crew bosses downtown, they'd acted hurried and tight-lipped as if they were anxious to get back into the woods. And the thirsty drill crews who had provided the nine o'clock town with what meager nightlife it enjoyed, had not shown up at all." Actually, Timmins' night life is so meager that it has more taverns and cocktail lounges per capita than any other town or city in Canada.

What Bragagnolo did not reveal was that in hiring teams of stakers to claim land near the Texas Gulf find he had two partners. One was John Angus, manager of one of the local brokerage firms. The other silent partner was Ken Darke.

As Darke explained it later, the partnership came about in early January. Bragagnolo, like Darke, had an intense interest in the penny stock market, and the two men frequently encountered each other in Angus's brokerage office.

> Mr. Bragagnolo approached me some time in January as I recall. He discussed the fact that rumors were spreading at that time that Texas Gulf had made a major discovery in the general vicinity, and he was interested in staking in that area. . . . Since we had become a little more friendly then, he asked me whether I would like to join him in this venture.

Darke swore that he had refused to give Bragagnolo any

information about the rumored Texas Gulf discovery. In entering the partnership with Bragagnolo and Angus, he also stipulated that he could not allow his private affairs to conflict with his position as an employee of Texas Gulf. Therefore, Bragagnolo, who was to arrange for the physical staking of the claims, was told to stay away from properties that were desired by Texas Gulf.

The net effect of this arrangement was that Bragagnolo could stake on behalf of the partnership only those areas which Texas Gulf had investigated and had found to give no indication of containing evidence of mineral content. It was property discards such as these that brought a total of between $1 and $2 million from penny mining companies. For the promoters of these companies, the claims were a bargain at any price: They were relatively close to the Texas Gulf discovery site, and the promoters expected to resell them at a handsome profit to their own shareholder-owned companies.

The financial arrangements of the partnership were vague from the beginning. What rough accounts there were were kept by Bragagnolo. There was no written agreement; the partners simply contributed enough cash to pay for the labor of claim-stakers, which generally came to about $30 or $35 for each of the 230 claims that the trio staked by the time the Texas Gulf discovery was announced.

"I don't think," Darke said later, "we probably put up more than two or three thousand dollars apiece."

The discovery of the Kidd Creek mine has always been represented by Texas Gulf's management as a "team effort," and no doubt it was. In the five years between the time Walter Holyk first suggested the project and hired Leo Miller to conduct his broad investigation of the Canadian Shield to the day Darke spotted K-55-1, there were perhaps a dozen Texas Gulf exploration people who narrowed the area of interest to Kidd-55. One of these was George Podolsky, who typically,

KEN DARKE MAKES HIS PRIVATE FORTUNE   99

as a member of the exploration department, was a Canadian. Podolsky is the same age as Ken Darke.

It is difficult to believe that Texas Gulf would have discovered the Kidd Creek mine without the efforts of Darke and Podolsky. The latter conducted photography and other aerial surveys of the ground around Timmins in 1959, 1960, and 1961. Walter Holyk, who played a key part in the discovery as both the initiator and director of the entire project, is, however, not overly impressed by my interpretation of the importance of Darke's role. As he wrote me on May 26, 1969: "I got the distinct impression, however, from your [earliest] manuscript, that you are depriving me and a number of associates from a major professional accomplishment and are attributing the discovery to the persistence and stubbornness of Ken H. Darke, without the support or knowledge of his superiors in Texas Gulf Sulphur. Nothing is farther from the truth and, in actual fact, Ken Darke's role, while contributing to the eventual discovery was largely mechanical in nature."

Ken Darke graduated from the University of British Columbia in 1956 with the degree of geological engineer. During his school years he had worked on mining projects throughout British Columbia, Alberta, and the Yukon. Darke was a field man, and he shucked every opportunity that would put him behind a desk.

Darke and Podolsky were together in May of 1958, when Texas Gulf first began to chart its mineral prospects on a northern peninsula of Baffin Island north of Hudson Bay. The supply source was Foxe Main, a government defense station situated on the mainland. In a chartered DC-3, Darke and Podolsky set out on May 14 to carry supplies to the peninsula campsite. Podolsky sat in the tail of the plane, his feet propped up against the boxes of cargo. Darke stood in the cockpit between the pilot and co-pilot; he was the only member of the crew familiar with the unmapped topography. About 60 miles from the destination, there was complete cloud cover. The pilot began his descent.

When the co-pilot suggested that the plane should regain altitude, Darke noticed that the altimeter read 3,800 feet. He knew there were mountains higher than that in the region. Before he could utter a warning, there was a slight bump; it was not enough to knock Darke from his feet, and the reaction of the plane was not even severe enough to awaken Podolsky back in the tail. But when Darke glanced back through the plane, one side of the fuselage was a sheet of flame. The DC-3 had hit the flat top of a mountain that would later be named Mount Podolsky. The pilot opened both engines, but that faint bump had removed both propellors. When the plane crashed a mile away, Podolsky was thrown clear from the tail. The fuselage was upside down and burning, and the fuel sizzled in the snow. Podolsky dragged the pilot and co-pilot from the wreckage, but Darke's feet had pierced the fuselage; he was stuck like a cork from the waist down.

Darke's back was broken, he had a severely injured jaw, and jagged metal tore his ear half off when he was pulled from the wreckage. Podolsky's ankles were both dislocated, but among the four men he was the only one who could move. For 87 hours they lay in the snow until rescue came. Podolsky was acclaimed for keeping his three colleagues alive. Darke returned to his home in Trail, British Columbia, where he convalesced for the remainder of the summer and prepared a paper on "type situations" where mineral deposits might be found in the Canadian Shield.

It was precisely in one of those "type situations" that Kidd-55 was found.

*

One of the mining promoters who was anxious to buy land from the Bragagnolo-Darke-Angus trio was 28-year-old Pasquale Giardine, a boyhood friend of Bragagnolo who had moved to Toronto to make his fortune in the brokerage business. Pat Giardine had not been a great success as a stock salesman. After three years as a customer's man with a member firm of the Toronto Stock Exchange, Giardine had several judgements outstanding against him. His financial position, he admitted, "was less than nil." He nevertheless incorporated his own private investment firm in the summer of 1963, and sought to buy control of small mine exploration companies listed on the Toronto Stock Exchange. His stake was $50,000, consisting of a $40,000 loan from a plumber friend and $10,000 from his father, a Timmins surgeon.

Through friends on Bay Street he found a dormant exploration company called Bunker Hill Extension Mines Ltd. Such was the state of the company that its shares were under suspension by the Toronto Stock Exchange. Bunker Hill had between six and seven thousand dollars in its treasury, and its main asset was the right to certain mining claims of undetermined value in Duprat Township, Quebec. Giardine paid $15,750 for 175,000 shares of Bunker Hill, an amount which represented the controlling interest. Although the company had more than two million shares outstanding, most of the shareholders were scattered and long ago disillusioned. Only a small percentage of shares was required to exercise control. On the market Bunker Hill shares were selling for 10¢.

In February of 1964 Giardine came into contact with his old friend, Ned Bragagnolo. Bragagnolo suggested a trip to Timmins, and the two men met in the basement of Giardine's father. Bragagnolo's proposition was 12 claims for $10,000 and 50,000 shares of Bunker Hill. "Ned said to me these properties were well located, due to the fact there was going to be a large American company announce a very important find."

This meeting took place in February, 1964, more than six

weeks prior to the announcement of the Texas Gulf discovery.

Giardine agreed to buy the 12 claims, about which he knew nothing other than that they were well located in relation to the Texas Gulf find. He was concerned only with the fact that Bragagnolo told him ". . . a large American company was going to make a very important discovery announcement." Giardine was quite candid about his own ignorance concerning mining matters. He once admitted that even a simple government geological survey map would have meant nothing to him.

Five days after meeting with Bragagnolo, Giardine arranged to transfer the claims from his own investment company to Bunker Hill. On behalf of his personal company, which had paid $10,000 plus 50,000 Bunker Hill shares for the claims, the agreement was signed "P. C. Giardine." On behalf of Bunker Hill, which was to pay $10,000 plus 300,000 shares, the agreement was signed "P. C. Giardine." The Toronto Stock Exchange balked at this proposed deal and insisted that Giardine should not make a profit at the expense of the shareholder-owned company that he controlled. The deal was amended so that Giardine would not personally profit at the expense of his own Bunker Hill shareholders.

Bunker Hill next needed the report of a mining engineer on its new claims. Giardine knew of no one, but through a mutual acquaintance found someone willing to survey the property. The 12 claims held such little promise that the engineer recommended preliminary work that would cost less than $1,900. On this basis, Bunker Hill raised $40,000 by selling 400,000 new treasury shares through the Toronto Stock Exchange.

Bunker Hill shares were reinstated for trading on the Toronto Stock Exchange and at first sold for prices between 10¢ and 15¢. Within two months, the stock rose to above $1 per share and the company had raised several hundred thousand dollars from the public by the sale of new shares. Most of this money went not into exploration, but into the purchase of Texas Gulf shares. Bunker Hill bought 6,000 shares of Texas Gulf during March and April, and sold the shares in May for a profit of $140,825.89

Giardine's father also made substantial purchases of Texas Gulf shares before April 16. Why would Bragagnolo, who stood to profit from this confidential knowledge, pass on news of the discovery to Giardine's father? "Well," said Pat Giardine, "a year or two prior to this particular situation Mr. Bragagnolo suffered an acute appendicitis. My father . . . did an emergency operation on Mr. Bragagnolo. Mr. Bragagnolo was very grateful for this and I believe this was one of the reasons he told my father."

Mainly as a result of the issue of treasury shares during and after the Timmins excitement, Bunker Hill Extension Mines found itself with net liquid assets of more than $620,000 at April 31, 1965. Three years later, after most of these liquid assets had left the company's treasury to pay for property acquisitions and exploration work, it was announced to shareholders that Pat Giardine was resigning as president and director due to the "pressure of other commitments." About all Bunker Hill had to show for the expenditure of that $600,000 or so was an interest in an Australian property which was producing very modest amounts of lead. For this interest, Bunker Hill advanced more than $225,000.

The public flocked to buy shares in companies such as Bunker Hill. Darke, knowing the land sold by himself and his partners to the penny mining companies held little promise of commercial ore, followed a practise of selling short. He made a profit of $42,706.82 trading and selling his Bunker Hill shares.

Ken Darke disclosed his private activities to Texas Gulf after the April 16 announcement of the discovery. He was given a leave of absence and submitted his resignation June 1, to be effective a month later. He married an attractive young widow whom he had met in the T. A. Richardson and Sons brokerage office, and established his own consulting firm in Timmins. At first he was besieged by mining promoters who wanted to use on their engineering reports the name of the man who spotted the Texas Gulf discovery hole. Darke and Bragagnolo became partners one last time in late 1964, when they acquired five square miles of concessions in New Guinea. "There are millions of tons of copper there," Bragagnolo said as the two men departed. Nothing came of the New Guinea venture, and Darke and Bragagnolo became estranged.

Bragagnolo moved to Montreal to devote all his time to the promotion of mining stocks.

John Angus, who had financed his share of the claimstaking trio with an $800 loan from his mother, was charged and acquitted of swearing a false declaration in connection with his acceptance of treasury shares for the sale of claims to Bunker Hill. At this writing he is studying at Laurentian University in Sudbury and plans to become a lawyer.

The total profit made by the partnership trio has never been disclosed and probably never will be. However, it is known that the three received $900,000 in cash for the sale of claims plus an undisclosed probably larger sum in mining shares. In addition to the partnership profits there were other huge profits made individually in stock trading.

On March 31, 1964, Ned Bragagnolo bought 2,000 shares of Texas Gulf stock at $26 per share and also purchased a six month call on another 2,000 shares. He has not revealed how long he held these purchases or how much he made, but by the end of September when the calls ran out, the paper profit was over $130,000.

Ken Darke did equally well. On February 20, 1964, he purchased 300 shares of Texas Gulf stock at 24⅛. One week later he approached a Timmins friend, T. F. Moran, who was working in a dry-cleaning plant. At Darke's request, Moran purchased a call on 1,000 shares of Texas Gulf stock at 22⅝ through an uncle who worked in a Montreal brokerage firm.

On March 30 and 31 Darke purchased options on another 2,000 shares at $24¾. When the options on the 3,000 shares ran out in the fall of that year, the paper profit was over $90,000. If he had chosen to exercise his calls and hold the stock he would have an additional $120,000 profit today.

Chapter Ten

THE MINE IS PROVEN

March 27 was Good Friday, and Texas Gulf had completed the staking of the last claim in its land acquisition program north of Timmins. From almost a standing start fewer than five months before, Ken Darke and his teams of stakers had cut their way through the bush and muskeg around the boundaries of nearly 250 claims. Save for a four-claim group in Prosser Township, Texas Gulf had every piece of land in the area that it desired, every plot where there was an anomaly that Hugh Clayton had pinpointed as worthy of investigation.

Chief Geologist Walter Holyk had been in Timmins infrequently since the drilling of K-55-1. On each occasion it was his habit to stay three or four days. But almost daily during those winter months there was communication between Timmins and the New York head office of Texas Gulf, and just as often Holyk reported to Mollison on the staking program.

There was no suggestion to this point that Texas Gulf or its officers had any duty whatsoever to disclose their Timmins activities to shareholders or to the public. It is a clearly accepted principle that the responsibility of management to the corporation goes far beyond the responsibility to any individual shareholder. Certainly there was a corporate purpose to be served in maintaining, for as long as necessary, secrecy about the results of K-55-1 and secrecy about the subsequent attempts to marshal choice land in the area.

It would have been impossible, or at least prohibitively expensive, for Texas Gulf to get rights to this land if it had been known that the Kidd Property had yielded a rich core. The intensity of the land acquisition campaign itself would have inspired the owners of privately owned land to drive a stiffer bargain, and would have brought speculators and representatives of other mining companies into the competition.

Easter Monday can be specified as the point in time when the land program was complete, for it was on that day that Earl Huntington, the member of Texas Gulf's legal department, was finally able to consummate an agreement to purchase rights to the Roberts property, which lay immediately to the south of Kidd 55. With that acquisition Texas Gulf now owned the one square mile whose four half lots had formerly belonged to the Hendrie, Roberts, and Elliott estates and the T. S. Woollings Company. It was this square mile of swamp and muskeg, later known as the "Kidd segment," that comfortably contained every part of the Kidd 55 anomaly.

In the more distant region, the land program had been conducted with some haste after the beginning of February. Walter Holyk was on one of his periodic trips to Timmins when Darke approached him about an important matter. Holyk had no inkling that Darke, in partnership with two Timmins men, was conducting his own staking program for his own private ends. Holyk later recalled that conversation with Darke:

> I believe it was in February when he mentioned to me that some acquaintance of his told him that he was in a bar and he sat in on a conversation wherein people at the bar were certain that we had encountered some mineralization and, regardless of what anybody thinks, that they were going to go in and stake some claims, and this acquaintance apparently told Darke that he was going to stake same claims.
>
> I believe this acquaintance is the chap who was subsequently identified as Bragagnolo, which I did not know at the time. But I can recall we were staggering our staking so as not to focus attention on the Kidd-55 area, because there were rumors around and we felt that we would prejudice our efforts to acquire the land if the promoters or the mining companies heard about it.
>
> So I at that time told Ken to go right into the Kidd-55 area and to stake all the claims that we need and to steer away his acquaintance, give him a helicopter ride or anything, just to get him out of the way.

Towards the end of March, it was becoming urgent to make plans for the resumption of drilling. The water plateau at Kidd-55 was close to the surface of the ground, and the spring thaw would make the terrain wet and greasy and all but impassable. If drill rigs and other heavy equipment were to be dragged to Kidd 55, it had to be done shortly.

Elsewhere there was good news for the 64,918 shareholders of Texas Gulf. The annual report for the year 1963 reported that sales had grown 5.56% to the highest total in four years. Sulphur, of course, still accounted for most of the company's revenues, and there were signs that the oversupply in the sulphur market which had caused prices to drop was being eliminated. Free world consumption of sulphur had risen

6.5% in 1963, while production increased by only 1%. For the first time since 1916, United States consumption exceeded domestic production.

The enormous Lacq sulphur mine in France had been an important source of new supplies in preceding years, but now it was nearing capacity production. Only one new recovery plant was due to come into production in western Canada. Japan and Italy, two countries which had traditionally prohibited sulphur imports, abandoned their restrictive policies in 1963, and the Soviet Union for the first time imported sulphur from the free world. Sulphur prices, shareholders were told, "may increase to a more normal level."

Still earnings were down. Net profit fell from $12,137,298, equivalent to $1.21 per share in 1962, to $9,353,652 or 93¢ per share in 1963. One reason was that the company's *S.S. Marine Sulphur Queen* had been lost at sea without a trace. Another reason for the drop in earnings was that Texas Gulf was putting more of its money to work, divorcing itself further from the conservative policies that had marked the company's history. Some liquid assets were turned into more productive fixed assets, and the continuing process of diversification caused further expenses.

Texas Gulf had once prided itself on its debt-free position; now it was preparing to sell $55 million worth of long-term bonds.

President Claude Stephens said, "It is our belief that 1963 marks a turning point in your company's recent trend of declining earnings." Even Stephens couldn't have foreseen that Texas Gulf's net profit would increase more than sixfold during the next four years. Texas Gulf later made much of this apparent turn in fortunes and argued that with the broad scope of its overall operations and the fact that its 10 million shares were valued at $170 million, one drill hole was hardly the company's salvation.

Even with the benefit of hindsight, it is difficult to measure how 65,000 shareholders collectively would react to this mix of news. The sulphur picture was undoubtedly improving, but Texas Gulf's diversification program had not been without problems. Plans to begin production from the new potash mine in Moab, Utah, had been delayed for a year by an explosion in 1963 which killed 18 Texas Gulf workers. The company had arranged to buy 230,000 acres of oil and gas properties in western Canada from Delhi-Taylor Oil Company, but management was not confident it hadn't paid too high a price (a feeling which may explain why the price was not revealed in the annual report). The Baffin Island lead-zinc property was still at the drill test stage. Texas Gulf's new phosphate facilities in North Carolina were not yet in production. In Wyoming the company had embarked on a promising trona (soda ash) venture, but it had not been proved that the properties were even mineable.

There was one piece of intelligence which remained the privilege of only the tight little group centered in Texas Gulf's exploration department: The results of drill hole K-55-1, and the more timely knowledge that drilling was about to resume on the Kidd segment.

On March 30 Walter Holyk's wife bought 100 shares of Texas Gulf at $25.87 per share. Mrs. Holyk paid for the shares out of a $4,000 loan she had recently made from her father. Holyk later explained the motive for this and other stock market purchases:

> I bought the stock, but it didn't have anything to do with the drill hole.
>
> I bought the stock or my wife bought the stock because I thought that the sulphur price would be going up around that time. There was a lot of rumor to that effect.
>
> I think Texas Gulf had a lot going for it at that time. The sulphur situation was improving. We were scheduled

to bring into production a potash mine. We had acquired vast reserves of phosphate in North Carolina. We acquired, through competitive bidding, trona properties that I thought was one of the best trona areas. We acquired oil and gas rights from Delhi-Taylor in Alberta. We were drilling several wells in Alberta. One was offset from a previous producer which had vast reserves and we were hopeful we would find something there.

I think I was also prompted by the fact there were a lot of mergers taking place. It became a fashion for oil companies to acquire fertilizer companies. There was a lot of publicity about the food shortages, the increased use of fertilizer, which meant that certainly the situation for sulphur would improve because a large proportion of sulphur is used in fertilizers.

Various companies had been taken over by oil companies. I can recall two in particular that I had examined about a year earlier for the purpose of a proposed merger on our part. One was Virginia-Carolina. This was taken over by Socony-Mobil at twice the price of the stock. Smith Douglas was another company I had examined and this was being considered for a takeover by Kerr-McGee. It was eventually taken over by the Borden Company.

Other oil companies acquired other fertilizer companies, and as far as I was concerned, we were a prime candidate for a takeover by one of the oil companies, and when Cap Rieber [President Captain Rieber] bought shares for Barber Oil Company in late October, when this information became public it seemed to me somebody was readying for a takeover of Texas Gulf.

Holyk conceded that he was also motivated by the company's work near Timmins. "I certainly knew of the hole [K-55-1] and I was hopeful we would find something there, that we would find a mine there eventually. But we were certainly a long way from a mine on the basis of one drill hole."

The day the Holyks bought their 100 shares, Ken Darke and some of his acquaintances to whom he had recommended the purchase of Texas Gulf were also engaged in the stock market. Darke had been in periodic contact during the preceeding few months with an old girl friend, Nancy Atkinson, who now lived in Arlington, Virginia, and worked for the United States Department of Commerce. Miss Atkinson bought call options on 400 shares of Texas Gulf on March 30; her mother, Mrs. Madge Caskey of Vienna, Virginia, bought call options on 1,000 shares; her friend Stanley Westreich of Arlington bought 500 shares at $25.75 each; and Miss Atkinson's boss, Herbert Klotz, an assistant undersecretary in the Commerce department, bought calls on 2,000 shares.

In Toronto on March 3 Darke's brother, Ernest, bought a call on 500 shares at a price of 22⅝. He made a second purchase of a call on 200 shares at 25½, placing the order from the insurance office where he worked as an accountant. Another friend of Darke, Cameron Miller of Toronto, picked up calls on 1,000 shares.

Broker Paul MacNames was also a friend of Ken Darke, and MacNames made about $40,000 as a result of information from Darke. On May 12, 1969, he described it, "It was no secret that I was a friend of Ken Darke. I got a mortgage on my ex-wife's house and with the money I bought an option on 1,500 shares at a price of 22½. I exercised the options at 52½."

The practice of buying call options seemed to have afflicted a number of the persons who were privy to information about the Kidd 55 property. In their most respectable context, calls are used as a hedge against uncertainty, almost as a type of term insurance. Investors occasionally use put and call options to protect against radical changes in the market prices of their investment portfolios.

But calls are also a device to gamble on the future price of securities. A person buying call options on Texas Gulf shares in April of 1963 might have paid, say, $4 per share for a six-month option. This was equivalent to a straight wager that the price of Texas Gulf shares would rise by more than $4 within six months. People who buy calls with this motive do so because of short-term considerations; it is hardly conceivable that the Texas Gulf insiders who purchased calls were doing so to acquire a "proprietary interest" in the company.

As I wrote in my book, *Anyone Can Make a Million*, in January, 1966:

. . . 5% of option buying comes from employees, officers or directors of firms who may have information of a favourable nature concerning major progress or increases in profits, before such information is generally available to shareholders and the public. The advantage of buying options instead of stock is tenfold, for by laying out the same amount of money much higher profits can be made. In 1962 Shell Oil decided to expand in Canada by taking over the Canadian Oil Company. Canadian Oil was then trading for $35 per share, and the Shell board of directors had voted at their directors' meeting to offer the equivalent of $55 for every share of Canadian Oil.

At that time I was a partner in a firm which had sold large numbers of options to put and call brokers in previous years. Suddenly we were swamped with requests to buy thirty-day calls on Canadian Oil for which we were offered $3.50 per share, a huge sum considering that a ninety-five-day call normally would sell for about that figure. These orders all emanated from New York and were unlimited; that is, they offered to buy any size.

The advantage to the buyer was obvious. If he bought 1,000 shares of Canadian Oil, his outlay would be $35,000. When the offer was announced he would get $55,000 for his stock, making a $20,000 profit. On the other hand, if he were to spend the same $35,000 for options on Canadian Oil at $3.50 each, he could buy options on 10,000 shares, on which his profit would now be 10,000 x the rise in price of the stock: $16.50 or a profit of $165,000.

This is actually what did happen. Options were purchased on many thousands of shares. The profits were immense.

A more recent example caused considerable public furor. Texas Gulf Sulphur made a huge copper discovery near Timmins. The first hole was drilled in November, 1963. Between November, 1963, and March 30, 1964, a number of calls on Texas Gulf Sulphur stock were purchased by employees. A statement was made by the company on April 12, 1964, that the drilling was too preliminary to make a decision as to whether or not an ore body existed. On April 16 the company reported 25,000,000 tons of indicated ore. During this four-day period, no calls were purchased by insiders. The stock went from $20 to $80. The option purchasers could have made up to $60,000 for every $3,000 investment. If they had bought the stock, they would have made only $9,000 on the same investment.

The side bets made by the Holyks and by Darke and his acquaintances on March 30 were exquisitely timed and not only because of the prospect of further drill investigation of Kidd-55. Unwittingly, the transactions were executed the day before Texas Gulf announced a $2 per ton increase in the price of sulphur. This was hard news that was bound to affect the market price of Texas Gulf shares, and it did. Although the stock had already risen from $22 to $26 during March, it was to continue upwards another $2 per share in the ensuing week.

Chief Geologist Walter Holyk and Ken Darke were at the property when K-55-3 began drilling on the night of March 31. This was the second drill to be aimed into the Kidd-55 anomaly, and it would establish that K-55-1 had not drilled "down dip" – that is, through a wide but shallow body of ore. There was the worse danger, although hardly worth contemplating, that K-55-1 had bored through a narrow vein of ore, had drilled "down a pipe." (K-55-2, of course, was of no consequence to the evaluation of the K-55 anomaly. It was the decoy hole that had been drilled far to the north and east of the first hole.)

Hugh Clayton, a 42-year-old Welshman with impressive qualifications in geophysical engineering, had mapped the dimensions and some other physical characteristics of the anomaly. The shape of the anomaly defied description: "It was just a blob like beef or something," and it ran roughly in a north-south direction. The anomaly was about 1,200 feet long and about 400 feet wide, but Clayton's ground examination suggested that only about half the length was potentially a mine.

Back in November, Clayton and Darke had conferred with each other on the location of the first hole, K-55-1. They chose a point where the anomaly yielded the best conductivity, but this was perilously close to what they understood to be the southern boundary of the Hendrie property. K-55-1, then, was drilled about 200 feet north of that spot and almost exactly on the eastern boundary of the anomaly.

Clayton couldn't be sure whether there was one wide conductor running north and south, or whether there were three more slender and separate conductive zones contained within the anomaly. Clayton and Darke discussed the economics of the problem and whether to drill three steep holes, one into each strong conductive band, or whether to try to cut the three conductors with one angled drill hole.

It was Clayton's opinion that "we could cut three conductors for the price of one hole" by angling the drill from the eastern boundary of the anomaly.

> Drilling from the east side, the two conductors are fairly close so we stand a good chance of catching both of those at least in one hole and then we could continue to where we thought we might intersect the third conductor and if we missed, or didn't get anything at all there, we might move the [drill] machine over and put a short hole into the third conductor only.

Clayton and Darke were in disagreement over the angle at which the drill should be pointed. Clayton felt that a shallow angle, 45 degrees from the horizontal, would give the drill a better chance of penetrating the furthermost conductor. Darke feared that at this angle the drill might slide along the surface of bedrock and fail to penetrate. With Holyk's approval Darke chose to aim the drill more steeply, at a 60-degree angle from the horizontal.

Clayton returned to Timmins in March to conduct further ground geophysical surveys and to consult on the location of further drill holes on the Kidd 55 anomaly. It was decided that the second hole, K-55-3, would be placed on the western side of the anomaly, directly across from the first hole, K-55-1, and this hole would help to establish whether ore values persisted across the width of the anomaly.

Then Clayton boarded a plane bound for Toronto via New York. While in Toronto he telephoned T. A. Richardson and Sons, a stockbrokerage firm which specializes in mining securities, and ordered 60 shares of Texas Gulf.

"Well, I was passing through Toronto and I called my broker, and it was pay day and I know I had a little cash, and I bought the 60 shares somewhat on impulse."

K-55-3 was drilled easterly through the anomaly at an angle of 45 degrees. Daily, reports were made through Mollison to Fogarty, and on up to Stephens.

In the evening of April 1, Holyk transmitted to Senior Vice-president Fogarty his visual estimate of the ore content of the first 64 feet of core. The next day Mollison passed on to Fogarty his general observations of the core from K-55-3, and at the same time, Holyk's visual assays of the length from 164 feet to 192 feet. On April 3, a Friday, Fogarty was in Salt Lake City on a trip to inspect the company's potash installation at Moab, Utah. There, by telephone, he heard Holyk's assays for the core length from 192 feet to 345 feet, and also spent a few minutes conversing with Mollison.

This type of daily communication continued until April 7, when K-55-3 was completed at a depth of 876 feet. Visual estimates of the core indicated an average copper content of 1.12% and an average zinc content of 7.93% over 641 feet of the hole. (On April 8, James Scott of Toronto's *Globe and Mail* phoned TGS Vice-president C. Myers to check out rumors of a rich copper discovery. Myers told him that he knew nothing of any copper find.)

The average gross assay values indicated by K-55-3, without regard to any silver content, was $26.43 per ton at prices then prevailing for copper and zinc. Gross assay value is simply the worth of the core that has been found; it does not take into account the cost of extraction, the cost of separating the metals, and the cost of shipping. But the Kidd-55 property was ideal for the cheap open-pit mining method, there was no indication that the metallurgy would cause serious problems, and shipping routes were well established from Timmins. Ore with gross assay values of little more than $5 per ton had been profitably mined from properties with similar characteristics and locations

But geology is an inexact science. What Texas Gulf had discovered, in absolute terms, were two tubular-shaped lengths of core, with rich metal values extending over 600 feet in each case. It would be absurd to suggest that the surrounding terrain, except for those lengths of core 1⅛ inches in diameter, was barren land. On the other hand, it would have been presumptuous to project the mineral values over the entire area of the anomaly. Freak occurrences abound in rock structure; what made K-55-1 and K-55-3 especially tantalizing was that the high ore values in each hole extended for 600 feet – about the length of two football fields.

Mining engineers for the Securities and Exchange Commission later contended that ore values persisted in an east-west line from K-55-3 to K-55-1 to a width of 373 feet. They further argued that, even if the ore values were present for only six inches on either side of that east-west line, Texas Gulf had already found ore worth $750,000.

Benjamin Adelstein, the SEC's chief mining engineer, said it was most difficult to imagine that such rich ore would not extend for at least some distance north and south of the east-west plane established by K-55-1 and K-55-3. "However, it is not possible to prepare an estimate of ore reserves at this time since mining engineering practice demands that volume be proven by a third drill hole, at least in a third dimension."

That third dimension was established by the third hole drilled into the Kidd-55 anomaly, designated K-55-4. The drilling began April 7 at 7 p.m., as soon as the rig could be moved from the location of K-55-3. It was placed 200 feet to the south of the first hole, K-55-1. K-55-4 confirmed the existence of a third dimension. It was completed in three days, by seven o'clock in the evening of April 10, and it encountered mineralization over 366 feet of its 579-foot length. Visual estimates indicated an average copper content of 1.14% over the mineralized portion, and 8.24% zinc.

Drill hole K-55-4 went out of worthwhile mineralization 24 hours before, at the 420-foot level, at 7 p.m., on April 9. This was a highly significant time and date, because, for the first time, Texas Gulf had a firm indication – if not proof – that the orebody was in three dimensions.

It was at this point the SEC said that Texas Gulf had truly discovered a mine. Assuming continuity of ore among the three drill holes, Adelstein estimated that drilling had established 7.7 million tons of ore averaging 1.15% copper, 8.14% zinc, with a gross assay value per ton of ore of $26.51 per ton. The gross value of this projected orebody was $204.2 million.

In the subsequent trial of 13 Texas Gulf employees on charges of insider trading, Judge Dudley Bonsal of the southern district of New York decided that Texas Gulf's exploration prior to seven o'clock on the evening of April 9 was not material. Until that time, he ruled, the company had yet to establish the probability that a body of commercial ore existed.

Before that time, therefore, he held that any information emanating from Kidd-55 was not "material" in the sense that it might have been expected to substantially affect the market price of Texas Gulf shares. (Bonsal's ruling on this matter was later reversed by the Court of Appeals.)

During the eight days that K-55-3 and K-55-4 were drilling to determine the second and third dimensions of the orebody, Senior Vice-president Charles Fogarty bought 800 shares, half of them at $26.50 each on April 1, and the other 400 shares at prices between $26.12 and $26.87 on April 6. Hugh Clayton bought 100 shares at $26.87 on April 2, and Mrs. Mollison, wife of the exploration manager, purchased 100 shares at $28.12 on April 8.

At the same time, Fogarty in discussions with President

Claude Stephens formulated tentative plans to announce the progress of drilling at K-55 at the annual meeting of shareholders scheduled for April 23 in Houston at the company's principal office. Still, no word of the discovery was passed onto the non-exploration members of management, and even David Crawford, Texas Gulf's secretary and manager of public and government relations, flew from New York to Houston to plan the physical set-up of the annual meeting without being aware of developments at Kidd 55.

Richard D. Mollison, manager of the exploration department, was directly responsible to the New York head office for the activities at Kidd 55. Mollison had been at the property until the morning of April 10, was aware of drilling progress until at least the night before, and was reporting on a current basis to Fogarty.

During his stay in Timmins, Mollison had continued to be subjected to inquiries from the *Northern Miner*, a trade publication based in Toronto. A *Northern Miner* reporter, Graham Ackerley, had heard the rumors originating in Timmins, and had been pressing Mollison for News. On April 6, Mollison on his own initiative invited Ackerley to visit the Kidd 55 property. By letter the same day, Mollison made arrangements for Ackerley to visit the property April 20, three days before the Texas Gulf annual meeting.

The timing was important. If Ackerley arrived at the Kidd property April 20, a Monday, it meant that his first report of Texas Gulf's activities could not be reported until the *Northern Miner* issued its regular weekly publication on April 23, a Thursday. And Thursday, April 23, was the date of the annual meeting at which Texas Gulf meant to release the results of drilling activities at Timmins. It was important that shareholders be told the news first hand, before learning of it through the news media.

On April 10 the *Toronto Telegram* reported: "Richard D.

Mollison . . . told the *Telegram* the Company is drilling in Kidd township, is looking for non-ferrous metals, but has made no copper discovery. He denied rumors of a copper strike by the company." That same day the *Toronto Star* reported, "The two Toronto brokerage houses with offices in Timmins have been deluged with local buying orders. Those who make it their business to know such things say Texas Gulf men have been big purchasers."

Chapter Eleven

THE INSIDERS

Until the New Deal, when Congress passed into law the Securities Exchange Act of 1934, American society looked on with tacit approval as corporate directors and officers enriched themselves in the stock market at the expense of their own minority shareholders. These stock market profits made by insiders with the use of advance confidential corporate information were looked upon as part of the emoluments of holding office. Indeed, many, if not most, of America's great fortunes accumulated at the end of the 19th century and the beginning of the 20th were built with information – about pending government contracts, disasters, wars, new inventions or techniques – that was not available to the public at large.

The Securities Exchange Act of 1934 didn't prohibit all

insider profits. It did, however, require that all insiders (directors, officers, and owners of more than 10% of a company's common shares), make public every month the full extent of their trading in their company's securities.

Congress also ruled that any "short-swing" profits made by insiders as a result of the purchase and sale of a stock or other security within six months should be returned to the corporation. In enacting this law, it was recognized that directors and officers of a corporation are servants of the shareholders: Their objective in owning a share of the corporation should be that of obtaining a "proprietary" and lasting interest. There was the additional consideration that insiders attempting to benefit from hot, confidential information would generally do this by aiming for short-term profits.

As in the Texas Gulf case, government prosecutions of alleged insider abuses have been conducted under Section 10 of the Securities Exchange Act, which authorized the Securities and Exchange Commission to prescribe rules of behavior "necessary or appropriate in the public interest or for the protection of investors."

Acting under this authority, the SEC in 1942, promulgated Rule 10b-5, which provides:

It shall be unlawful for any person, directly or indirectly, by the use of any means or instrumentality of interstate commerce, or of the mails, or of any facility of any national securities exchange,

(1) to employ any device, scheme or artifice to defraud

(2) to make any untrue statement of a material fact or to omit to state a material fact necessary in order to make the statements made, in the light of the circumstances under which they were made, not misleading, or

(3) to engage in any act, practice or course of business

which operates or would operate as fraud or deceit upon any person, in connection with the purchase or sale of any security.

What the SEC set out to prove in its case against Texas Gulf was that information concerning the results of early drilling on the Kidd property was "material." This key word has been defined in a number of ways by the courts, one example being that material information is information "which in reasonable and objective contemplation might affect the value of the corporation's stock. . . ." When did the developments at Kidd Township reach the point that they would be expected to influence the price of Texas Gulf shares?

There was no reason why the price of Texas Gulf shares should have been affected by the aerial detection, in 1959, of the Kidd 55 anomaly. The company had discovered thousands of anomalies, and at least a handful gave as strong an electromagnetic reaction as Kidd 55. Besides, the anomaly only gave indication of conductive material in the ground; it could have been caused by worthless graphite. Even water conducts electricity.

Did the information from Kidd 55 become "material" after the core was pulled from the first hole, K-55-1?

The Securities and Exchange Commission said the core contained "such extraordinary values that it has been accurately described as the most impressive drill hole accomplished in modern times." The SEC contended that K-55-1 "opened to Texas Gulf the area of mining, developing, smelting and selling base metals such as copper and zinc and other more precious metals, such as silver, of an extraordinary value."

Without exception, the Texas Gulf employees who bought shares in the weeks and months following K-55-1 said they had acted not on the basis of the results from K-55-1. They all replied that they were prompted to buy shares by a firmer market for sulphur and by a general improvement in the fortunes of Texas Gulf. K-55-1 was "a good hole," said Walter Holyk. It was "an excellent hole," said Ken Darke. But there were other reasons for buying Texas Gulf shares.

Orison Marden, who acted for Texas Gulf at the ensuing insider trial, argued:

> . . . all that was known about this prospect was that there had been a single drill core, a single time to drill . . . you may be going right down the lead of a pencil; you may be going down a single vein. The vagaries and the contortions of mineralization are enormously varied, and nobody can tell. Is that "material" information that would significantly affect the value of 10 million shares of Texas Gulf Stock? . . .
>
> This single hole . . . could actually, far from being an asset, have been a real liability to the company. . . . This company has had instances where millions of dollars have been spent after first indications looked awfully good and they turned out to be duds.

(What Marden didn't mention was that on the basis of this single drill hole Texas Gulf had gone out and staked thousands of acres surrounding the property, using the utmost secrecy so as not to alert others to what they were doing.)

Geophysicist Hugh Clayton said he'd seen better drill cores elsewhere, and this assertion led to one of the most devastating exchanges of the trial. (His interrogator is SEC lawyer Frank Kennamer Jr.):

Q. What did you think of the hole?

A. It was a good hole, sir. It certainly isn't the wonderful thing that the press and the SEC have made it out to be.

Q. You never had seen a better hole?

A. Oh, yes.

Q. Mr. Clayton, how many drill holes in your experience

have you known that intersected ore values of approximately $30 per ton over a length of 600 feet, twice the length of a football field, and, I think, maybe twice [sic] the height of the Empire State Building?

A. Well, I can't mention any specific holes. Of course, in the first case you don't value ore by saying that its gross assay value is $30. I mean, that is not the value of the ore.

I have worked in mines – in fact, apart from the coal mines, I don't think I worked in any mines where the overall value of the ore was less than it is at Timmins or was in the first hole anyway; and in big ore bodies you naturally get long holes, but I can't remember any specific ones.

Q. Mr. Clayton, can you name one situation where you investigated or knew of a core recovered over a length of 600 feet bearing ore values in the neighborhood of $30 a ton. Just one, Sir.

A. Well, Sir, I worked, for example, at the Saint Eulalie mine [in Mexico] at the American Smelting and Refining Company, and the main orebody then that we were working on was, oh, hundreds of feet in all directions, and we did a lot of drilling there, of course, and I logged a lot of the core. I feel there must have been holes where the core is certainly much more valuable.

Q. Mr. Clayton, can you think of any exploratory drill core, running 600 feet in length, bearing ore values of $30, other than Kidd 55?

A. Well, not in length. Certainly we have had a good many holes where the material was more valuable.

Whatever influence K-55-1 might have had on the Texas Gulf insiders, the fact is that they invested nearly $100,000 in shares of their Company between November 12, 1963, and

April 1, 1964, when drilling was resumed. The SEC's contention that this was unfair to other shareholders was summed up at the trial: "This stock came from some source, and that source was necessarily the shareholders of the company, who were unarmed with that information."

By seven o'clock on the evening of April 9, the drill crew had passed through mineralization in the third hole to penetrate the Kidd 55 anomaly. Texas Gulf had yet to utter a public word about its exploration activities in Kidd Township. But rumors of the find were becoming intense, and the company was getting more frequent queries from Canadian newspapers. Within a week Texas Gulf was to be the sensation of the investment and mining worlds.

Chapter Twelve

THE TIPPEES AND THE OPTIONEES

Some time in the middle of November, Fogarty and Stephens enjoyed a casual lunch with Harold Kline, then the company's secretary and later to become its general counsel. Fogarty and Stephens, of course, were aware of the results of drill hole K-55-1, but Kline was quite ignorant of the exploration work north of Timmins. Kline remembered, "The conversation turned to a favorable development connected with the hole at Timmins, and there was a reference to a telephone call [from Ken Darke] which had communicated the word of the favorable development."

Kline was not an expert in the field of metals exploration. He enquired whether the sulphide mineralization discovered near Timmins was similar to that at Texas Gulf's other discovery areas in Baffin Island and in New Brunswick. He was told that "the mineralization involved a combination of the sulphur element with evidence of copper and zinc, which was similar in terms of composition to that at New Brunswick rather than the mineralogy at Baffin Island where the element sulphur combined with lead and zinc."

In mentioning the Timmins drilling, Stephens had contravened his own firm policy that Texas Gulf employees who were not members of the exploration group were to be kept in ignorance of Kidd 55. At the time, however, the company was preoccupied with acquiring the land surrounding the Kidd property, and it may have been that Kline's advice was sought on this matter. He remembers that it was mentioned at the luncheon that "drilling was right on the boundary and that we would be interested in acquiring more property so that further exploration could be conducted."

Until late February, when Kline was promoted to general counsel and became personally involved in the land acquisition program, this was the full extent of his information about the exploration in Kidd Township.

At Christmastime, 1963, Ken Darke took time off from his staking program to spend a few days with a girl friend in Washington, D.C.

During his extensive travels, Darke had once investigated a group of base metals claims in the Blue Hill area of Maine. Through a girl friend he met in Maine, Darke was introduced to Nancy Atkinson, who later became a secretary in the Commerce Department. This wasn't Darke's first visit to Miss Atkinson's home; he had visited and telephoned there a number of times. Nancy knew nothing about the stock market, but her mother, Mrs. Madge Caskey, was fascinated by it.

Mrs. Caskey had been an accounts analyst with a bank for 15 years. She carefully read the financial pages of the New York newspapers, and awaited the arrival of the *Northern*

Miner every Friday. As far as Darke was concerned, she says, "I remember, yes, discussing different stocks with him and he repeatedly advised me to buy Texas Gulf if I wanted to buy some stock." On one of these occasions Mrs. Caskey had bought "eight or ten shares" of Texas Gulf. She swore afterwards that Darke had never discussed the company's activities near Timmins. "I knew he was in Canada, but I didn't know what he was doing."

Barely had Darke departed from Washington when Mrs. Caskey bought calls on 300 shares of Texas Gulf, giving her an option to buy the stock over a future period at $22.25. She had never bought call options before. "The idea came from an article in the newspaper which I had read which described puts and calls. I had never even heard of it before that."

The extent of Nancy Atkinson's previous experience in the stock market had been the purchase of a few shares of American Telephone and Telegraph. According to her own recollection, Nancy had been impressed with Darke's repeated advice to invest in Texas Gulf. "He had been with the company for some time and had many, many times spoken well of the company, and that it [the stock] was advancing right along, and he was always most enthusiastic about Texas Gulf." Nancy decided to buy the stock, and sought the advice of a family friend, Stanley Westreich, a real estate dealer in nearby Arlington, Virginia.

"I originally asked him if he had heard of the stock, and that I was thinking about buying some – I knew my mother had – and asked his opinion of what he thought about it. He said he didn't know very much, but he would check into it, and he did and he seemed to feel that the company was gaining at a nice pace and it would seem to be a pretty sound company, and I assume he looked into all the details of the company." Nancy took six weeks to make up her mind. On February 17 she bought calls on 200 shares of Texas Gulf, exercisable at a price of $23.12. The same day Westreich bought calls on 1,000 shares at prices exercisable at between $23.25 and $23.62.

One day while Nancy was discussing the Texas Gulf investment with her mother, she was overheard by Herbert Klotz, an undersecretary in the Commerce Department. Klotz had been in the investment banking business, but joined the government as a result of working in the 1960 presidential campaign for John F. Kennedy. Klotz overheard the conversation "simply by chance."

> "I couldn't help but listen to her side of the conversation. At the conclusion of the phone conversation, Miss Atkinson told me she had been speaking to her mother, who had advised her she was going to add to her previous investment in Texas Gulf stock. She told me that she, too, was going to add to her previous investment in Texas Gulf.

Klotz remembered that Nancy had mentioned she had an acquaintance who was employed by Texas Gulf, but that was all. What impressed Klotz about the company was:

> There was considerable talk in the papers about an increase in the price of sulphur. There had been substantial advances in the prices of some of the other sulphur stocks. I don't recall Miss Atkinson had any other information, except she thought this – and, of course, she also had her own experience of seeing her own investment going up in value.

Klotz bought calls on 2,000 shares of Texas Gulf on March 30 and 31, the day before the company was to resume drilling on its Kidd Township property. That same day, Nancy Atkinson bought calls on another 400 shares, Mrs. Caskey bought calls on an additional 1,000 shares, and Stanley Westreich bought 500 shares outright at $25.75 each.

Dr. Frank Smolarczyk graduated from medicine in Austria in 1943, and joined the German Navy. After the war he emigrated to Canada and came to live in Timmins. For the three years until he was able to get his Canadian medical license, he worked as an underground miner at Pamour Porcupine Mines.

In 1955, Dr. Smolarczyk finally got his licence to practise and became a general practitioner in Timmins. His office was directly upstairs from John Angus's brokerage house and soon he and Angus were close friends. When Angus introduced Smolarczyk to Darke, they immediately hit it off. The doctor, however, did not become friendly with the other physicians in town, who disliked his socialistic views and took every possible opportunity to harass him.

During his years as a general practitioner in Timmins, Dr. Smolarczyk made a considerable sum of money investing in the local blue chip stocks, Ventures and Falconbridge, and by the end of 1963 he had a substantial portfolio. He now sold everything and began to purchase Texas Gulf Sulphur stock, which was then trading at $24.00 a share. He continued to buy as the stock rose, and months later he sold it all at $72 a share. He then exultantly said to the local member of parliament, Murdo Martin, "At last I'm financially independent. Now I'm going to go up to that hospital and tell those doctors to kiss my Royal Canadian."

As Smolarczyk described it to me, "It was the opportunity of a lifetime. The miners who were my patients were also my friends because I had worked underground with many of them. I got my first tip from a driller at another company and my best friend John Angus didn't confirm it until I twisted his arm. I ended up making $450,000.00."

Dr. Smolarczyk went back to Austria, spent two years

studying psychiatry and then returned to Canada where he practised his specialty in Brockville. He never sold his Timmins home and his tenant is now a Timmins consulting geologist, one Ken Darke.

On February 20, 1964, Harold Kline was appointed general counsel to Texas Gulf Sulphur Company. Being the third Thursday of the month, it was the day of the company's regular board meeting, but first there was a meeting of the stock option committee, which comprised three directors whose duty it was to consider the granting of incentive stock options to company employees according to the recommendations of President Stephens. One of the committee members was not in New York; the two-man quorum was constituted by Francis Coates, the Houston lawyer, and John Hill, another non-management director who was the chairman of Air Reduction Company and director of a number of other companies. It was not company policy to grant options to employees who had not reached the status of company officer, but in this case, Stephens had recommended that Walter Holyk, the chief geologist, metals division, and four other employees be candidates. Holyk barely met the $24,000 salary minimum which was also generally required to qualify for stock options.

Neither Hill nor Coates was aware of Kidd 55. Hill said, "I had never heard of the Timmins area."

This meeting was something of a revival for the committee. Incentive options had not been granted for two years, partly because the price of Texas Gulf shares had reached such a dismal level that Stephens and Fogarty were fearful that the granting of further options would bring on the wrath of shareholders. Now the price was back to its 1961 level, and besides, Stephens and Fogarty had reason to maintain the allegiance of certain of their employees. The committee members, Coates and Hill, approved the granting of options to a sizeable number of Texas Gulf employees at the prevailing New York Stock

Exchange price. Among that group were Stephens, with options on 12,800 shares; Fogarty, 7,300 shares; Mollison, 4,300 shares, Kline, 4,300 shares; and Holyk, 2,000 shares. The full board of directors gave its blessing.

All the options were to buy Texas Gulf stock at $23.81. Within three months these optionees had a million-dollar paper profit. The options become worth over $3½ million in a little over a year. Strangely enough, some of them were never exercised.

Chapter Thirteen

APRIL 12

In the week preceding Sunday, April 12, Texas Gulf President Claude Stephens noticed with some concern that his company's shares were trading more actively and the price was creeping higher. He did his best to ignore the rumors that were filtering down from Canada, relying on his theory that rumors not widely publicized in the press "have little, if any, effect on the market."

The *Northern Miner* had got wind of the stories. Texas Gulf management was contemplating an announcement concerning its Kidd Township exploration at the April 23 shareholders' meeting, and it was important that any disclosures not be made in the *Northern Miner* before the shareholders were given details at the annual meeting.

While these plans were being incubated at Texas Gulf, disaster struck. The April 9 morning edition of the Toronto *Globe and Mail* published a story about the discovery rumors. James Scott, the paper's mining editor, wrote:

> Rumors that one of the biggest copper deposits in North America has been discovered near Timmins have Bay Street agog.
>
> Shares of penny mining companies with properties in the area have been trading in the millions of shares and their prices have been doubling and trebling.
>
> Yesterday's addition to the list of companies with properties in the district was PCE Explorations Ltd., which doubled in price to 25 cents a share while trading 1,232,465 shares.

The *Globe and Mail* story then quoted the president of PCE Explorations to the effect that his company was acquiring claims near holdings of Texas Gulf.

> He [the PCE president] said there was no definite reason for the acquisition, "but where there is smoke there is fire."
>
> This remark was a reference to the rumors that Texas Gulf has made a discovery of extreme importance. The company is working in the area but officials decline to confirm or deny the rumors.
>
> Kenneth Darke, engineer in charge of Texas Gulf's operations in the area, referred queries to the head office in New York. Telephone calls to C. O. Stephens, president of Texas Gulf, were fruitless. A Vice-president, C. Myers [probably marketing vice-president A. N. Myers] said he knew nothing about a copper discovery.
>
> But lending credence to the rumors was the fact that Texas Gulf employees in Timmins have been heavy

buyers of the company's stock through brokerage offices in that town.

Also lending support is the action of Texas Gulf shares on the New York Stock Exchange which yesterday rose $1.62 a share to a record $29.62. In the past two weeks the price has risen more than $5 a share. While the New York market has been strong in recent weeks, the Texas Gulf advance far exceeds the market's average rise in the two-week period.

The *Toronto Daily Star*, meanwhile, had dispatched a reporter to Timmins to check out the rumors. On the same day the *Globe and Mail* story appeared, he reported back:

Rumors gained ground here today of a major copper strike about 10 miles north of Timmins by Texas Gulf Sulphur Co. of New York.

Company officials refused to comment.

The rumors have been circulating for several weeks in stock market circles but a company spokesman said earlier there was nothing yet to indicate the existence of a commercial orebody.

Ken Darke, project engineer, said here Wednesday: "I have no statement whatever to make."

. . . One source said high copper values have been obtained but it was much too early to put a tonnage estimate on the discovery.

These news reports were quickly transmitted to New York by telephone and Telex. The next day, April 10, 92,100 shares of Texas Gulf changed hands on the New York Stock Exchange and the price closed at its high for the day of $30.12.

Claude Stephens decided the rumors could no longer be ignored. On the Friday afternoon of April 10, he telephoned

Thomas Lamont, the senior member of Texas Gulf's board, to seek advice.

> I asked Mr. Lamont if he had heard or read any of the rumors that were emanating from Canada with regard to Texas Gulf's exploratory program up there. And, as I recall, Mr. Lamont said he thought he had heard some rumors about what was supposed to be going on up there. He said, "Is there any truth in it?"
>
> I said, "We don't know. We need a little time to evaluate our program in this particular area. These rumors that are emanating from Canada are not correct, they are not and can't be substantiated by any of the work that has been done up to date. So I am concerned that the public and the stockholders may be getting the wrong information."
>
> And he asked me if it was in the press, I said it had been in the Canadian press.
>
> Then we talked on a bit about this problem and I asked Mr. Lamont if he had any advice with regard to what should be done or what I should do in this instance.
>
> Mr. Lamont replied by saying that if I didn't have anything to say of a definite nature that he would advise that nothing be said "until such time as you do have enough information to announce to the public what you have." But he said, "In any event, these rumors, so long as they stay in the Canadian papers, I think you may be able to live with them. But if they should get into the papers in the United States," he said, "it might be advisable to give the press an announcement with regard to the true situation."

This was the advice Stephens wanted to hear. In the atmosphere of uncertainty, he was loathe to issue a statement. Additionally, it was his strong wish that news of the Kidd

exploration should first be announced in the full-dress sur-
roundings of the annual meeting of shareholders, April 23.
That wish was to be thwarted by the events of the next day.

On the morning of April 11, the *New York Herald Tribune*
carried the first published report in the United States pertaining
to Texas Gulf's rumored discovery in Kidd Township. The
article, prominently displayed on the front page, contained
a number of inaccuracies. It read:

> The biggest ore strike since gold was discovered more
> than 60 years ago in Canada has stampeded speculators
> to the snowbound old mining city of Timmins, Ontario,
> some 450 miles northwest of Toronto. This time it's
> copper.
>
> Texas Gulf Sulphur Co. Ltd., which reportedly has
> made an unparalleled find in the Big Water Lake area
> about 15 miles north of Timmins would not confirm
> reports of the strike.
>
> . . . The richness of the copper it discovered was so
> great that samples reportedly were flown out of the
> country to be assayed. The huge lode is supposed to
> consist of a bed of copper sulphide 600 feet wide, with
> a possible overall copper return of 2.87 per cent through
> most of its width. This yield in itself is considered rich in
> mining circles.

And then there came the passage that made Vice-president
Charles Fogarty "exceedingly upset" and "very angry." It said:

> PCE Explorations reportedly is the company which
> worked with Texas Gulf Sulphur to make the strike.
>
> PCE Explorations, reportedly a key in the exploration
> work, slipped one cent to 46 cents [per share] after a huge
> rise of 22 cents on Thursday.

Fogarty had never before heard of PCE Explorations. He

immediately made inquiries about the company and found out that it was "a penny, speculative, wild Canadian flier." (Unknown to Fogarty at the time, PCE had acquired its stock market appeal because of a group of claims acquired near the rumored discovery at Kidd 55. PCE had acquired those claims from a private partnership in which a silent partner was Texas Gulf's Ken Darke.)

One of the first members of Texas Gulf's senior management to see the *Herald Tribune* story on April 11, was David M. Crawford, whose title was Secretary and Manager of Public and Government Relations. After some government experience and 13 years of corporate legal work with Socony Vacuum Oil Company and then Abbott Laboratories, Crawford had joined Texas Gulf in January, 1964. At the February 20, 1964, board meeting, he had been appointed secretary. In his new position, Crawford was responsible for the physical planning and organization of the annual meeting of shareholders which, in 1964, was scheduled for April 23 in Houston. Crawford had not seen the company's offices in Houston, nor had he met some of the Texas Gulf managers there. For these reasons, Crawford set out for Houston on the morning of April 11.

At Newark airport he bought a copy of the *Herald Tribune* while waiting for his flight, and to his surprise, saw the front page story about the Kidd Township discovery. Crawford didn't even know that Texas Gulf was exploring in Kidd Township. At about 11 a.m. he telephoned from the airport to the home of Texas Gulf President Claude Stephens in Connecticut. Stephens had not yet seen the article and asked Crawford to read it to him over the telephone.

Stephens wasted no time phoning his Senior Vice-president, Fogarty, the man with overall responsibility for all Texas Gulf's exploration. Fogarty hadn't seen the articles, as he was in the habit of buying the morning newspapers at the commuter station on his way to the office. He told Stephens he'd drive downtown in Rye, New York, get the *Herald Tribune* and *New York Times*, and then call Stephens back.

I called Mr. Stephens back and discussed the contents of the newspaper articles with him. The *Times* had also carried a story about the rumors of the Texas Gulf discovery. We were both quite upset. I was especially upset at these articles. Because certainly they were full of exaggerations and what I considered to be erroneous statements. . . . In my opinion they were exaggerated and could be misleading to the public.

Stephens, whose formal education led to a degree in petroleum engineering, had no experience in exploration for minerals; he relied wholly on Fogarty in this area.

When Fogarty had apprised himself of the newspaper articles, Stephens said that Texas Gulf would have to issue a press release to "clarify" the rumors. Fogarty agreed and telephoned Robert Carroll, a vice-president of Doremus and Company, the public relations firm that handled Texas Gulf's account. According to Fogarty's recollection Carroll was also of the opinion "that from a public relations point of view we had an obligation to make some statement."

The time was 12:30, Saturday, April 11. Dick Mollison, who had been on the spot in Timmins until the day before, had called Fogarty on his arrival in New York with a general report on drilling progress. Now Fogarty called Mollison again and asked for "a complete geological review, to give his expert opinion to me on what the situation was in Timmins."

"I asked him was there anything I didn't know about, were there any new developments, had he heard from anybody." Mollison had left the Kidd Township at around noon the day before, at which time the third hole – K-55-4 – had gone through mineralization.

For the next two or three hours, Fogarty sat at home, reviewing all the information at his disposal, reread the newspaper articles, and jotted down some ideas for a news release. "And then I would say about 4:30 or thereabouts I called Mr. Mollison again."

At his home in Old Greenwich, Connecticut, Dick Mollison awaited the arrival of Fogarty, who lived a ten-minute drive away. He knew the chemical assays from the first hole, and he had in his possession a geologist's log of the second core. The log of the third core was not complete. He checked off what he thought were the inaccuracies in the *Times* and *Herald Tribune* stories. The *Herald Tribune* story had mentioned the orebody had a width of 600 feet.

> At that time I didn't know what the width was. They, the stories, generally referred to copper and nickel, and we had no nickel. The assay and visual inspections that we had indicated that zinc was more prominent a good deal than copper. In general, the rumors were exaggerated and inaccurate.

Before the arrival of Fogarty some time between five and six o'clock, Mollison called the *Northern Miner*'s Graham Ackerley at his home in Toronto. He suggested to Ackerley that the proposed visit to the Kidd property be moved ahead, from April 20 to April 13.

> There were so many rumors we thought perhaps if the reporter [Ackerley] visited the place and saw whatever there was to see and wrote his own story, it might serve to clarify the situation because the rumors were quite fantastic, some of them, about the width of ore that there was.

Fogarty arrived and asked Mollison what conclusions could be drawn from the work at Kidd 55 and, more to the point, what conclusions could be expressed publicly. "The only conclusion I was willing to draw," Mollison said later, "was that we had to keep on drilling."

I thought it was impossible to understand what we had . . . with the limited work we had done, our lack of understanding of any structure, and my concept of the nature of the sulphide ore-bearing occurrences.

It was impossible at that time . . . to make projections from one hole to the other. I felt perhaps that we were something like three blind men and the elephant; I didn't know what we were poking at at the time.

I had in mind the closest known sulphide occurrence to this one that we were working on, one twelve miles away [the Kam Kotia mine], which was a series of small disconnected sulphide masses. I think there are probably a dozen or more of them in this other mine . . . and in a new situation, with no geology of our own – we were working through the muskeg, with no help from surface geology whatsoever, it was out in the middle of a swamp – it is necessary to try to get any help from the closest possible source.

Sulphide bodies are likely to have the same general habit in a district, and this other occurrence twelve miles away, the closest one, was extremely erratic, not only in the fact that there were a number of small, disconnected bodies but in the mineralization within these bodies.

I simply was unwilling to draw any specific conclusions as to what we had. I thought we should do more work before we tried to decide what we had. I told him [Fogarty] it was too early for us to define what we had.

Armed with these views, Fogarty returned to his home and sat at his kitchen table to write down what elements he thought should be included in the release. He then took a copy of these notes to Carroll, the public relations man, who also lived in Rye, New York. Carroll was to compose a statement suitable for release to the press. Fogarty was to pick up this draft statement on his way home from church the next day.

Fogarty felt the need for legal advice, and tried unsuccessfully to contact Harold Kline, Texas Gulf's general counsel, and David Crawford, the company's secretary. By nine in the evening he decided to call Earl Huntington, who worked in the company's legal department.

> We discussed the content [of the proposed release] and he quizzed me in some depth as to the status of things and the accuracy of things. . . . We discussed back and forth that we wanted to make as clear a statement as was humanly possible to the people so there wouldn't be any misunderstanding or misleading information. . . . He told me that as far as he was concerned, legally it was alright.

The next morning, Fogarty went to Carroll's home, where the release was being typed in the presence of some other representatives of Doremus and Company. With Carroll listening on a telephone extension, Fogarty called Stephens to read the final draft of the release. Stephens suggested no major changes, but instructed that the release should be distributed to the newspapers and wire services as soon as possible. He did suggest that since Fogarty had largely written the release, he should be named in it as the spokesman. It read:

> NEW YORK, April 12, 1964 – The following statement was made today by Dr. Charles F. Fogarty, executive vice-president of Texas Gulf Sulphur Company, in regard to the company's drilling operations near Timmins, Ontario, Canada. Dr. Fogarty said:
>
> "During the past few days, the exploration activities of Texas Gulf Sulphur in the area of Timmins, Ontario,

have been widely reported in the press, coupled with rumors of a substantial copper discovery there. These reports exaggerate the scale of operations, and mention plans and statistics of size and grade of ore that are without factual basis and have evidently originated by speculation of people not connected with TGS.

"The facts are as follows. TGS has been exploring in the Timmins area for six years as part of its overall search in Canada and elsewhere for various minerals – lead, copper, zinc, etc. During the course of this work, in Timmins as well as in Eastern Canada, TGS has conducted explorations entirely on its own, without the participation by others. Numerous prospects have been investigated by geophysical means and a large number of selected ones have been core-drilled. These cores are sent to the United States for assay and detailed examination as a matter of routine and on advice of expert Canadian legal counsel. No inferences as to grade can be drawn from this procedure. "Most of the areas drilled in Eastern Canada have revealed either barren pyrite or graphite without value; a few have resulted in discoveries of small or marginal sulphide ore bodies.

"Recent drilling on one property near Timmins has led to preliminary indications that more drilling would be required for proper evaluation of this prospect. The drilling done to date has not been conclusive, but the statements made by many outside quarters are unreliable and include information and figures that are not available to TGS.

"The work done to date has not been sufficient to reach definite conclusions and any statement as to size and grade of ore would be premature and possibly misleading. When we have progressed to the point where reasonable and logical conclusions can be made, TGS will issue a definite statement to its stock holders and to the public in order to clarify the Timmins project."

The government later charged that this press release was false and misleading and an attempt to deceive the public. Certainly if it was meant to cool down the stock market, it didn't have that immediate effect: On Monday morning, April 13, Texas Gulf shares traded at a seven-year high of $32.00.

Chapter Fourteen

THE NEWS IS RELEASED

At 2:30 Sunday afternoon, Fogarty drove Mollison and Walter Holyk to meet the airport limousine. Fogarty said his goodbyes and beseeched the two men to "move things along" at the Kidd property. The Air Canada flight from Toronto to Timmins arrived at about 10:30. Mollison and Holyk took a taxi the six miles downtown to the Bon Air Motor Hotel, where Darke was waiting with an up-to-the-minute briefing.

Darke and Holyk flew to the Kidd property first thing in the morning. In line with previous arrangements, Mollison picked up *Northern Miner* reporter Graham Ackerley outside the Empire Hotel at 10 a.m. and drove him to the helicopter pad. This was the first time Mollison had met Ackerley, a reporter with years of experience in mining.

At the property, the four men retired to the cook shack for a cup of coffee and a short discussion. Mollison remembered that Ackerley (who habitually droops a cigarette from the corner of his mouth) was impatient with talking. He wanted to see some drill core.

So we went over to the office tent where some of the core was in out of the weather and showed him some core there. He also saw plan maps of the drilling, and I believe that someone read to him a series of composite assays from drill hole number one [K-55-1].

It was Holyk, with assistance from Darke, who did most of the talking. Holyk showed Ackerley parts of the core from K-55-3 and gave him summaries of the status of drilling "as we knew it at that time." The discussion lasted about an hour, and Ackerley was invited to have lunch at the drill camp. There was a firm understanding that Ackerley could not release the article without Mollison's approval. In the meantime, the *Northern Miner* reporter was sworn to secrecy.

Some weeks later, Ackerley wrote his own highly dramatic account of that day:

Monday morning. Fly at 9:00. Last minute change. Make it 10:00, another hour of waiting. Finally a car pulls up, waving me in. To the airport. Right in to the chopper. Airborne. Ten minutes against a stiff headwind. And then, down below, five rigs working on a grid pattern. From the air it looks like a 200-ft. grid. That's it! They've got a big one! But silence from my escort, although he's wearing a grin that bisects his face from ear to ear.

Some quick handshakes. Ken Darke. Walt Holyk. All smiles no words, but come on down to the cookery for a cup of coffee. One cup. Two. Come on, have another! "The heck with you fellows – I've been waiting for weeks now, and I don't want to wait another minute." And so off down the camp. The birth of Dragon Town. The winter camp door is pushed open. NX core on the floor. Massive chalco, massive sphalerite. Not a word. Three steps in, a quick glance at the core. They said afterwards my hand shook. It probably did. The biggest thrill a man could ever experience.

Mollison said later:

He gave the article to me at my request, because he did not have freedom to publish the article at that time. He wrote the article with the understanding that it would be turned over to me and held until we were willing to let him publish. We made no attempt to censor or control what was written.

Mollison spent all day Tuesday, April 14, at the property, and on his return to Timmins was handed Ackerley's story. Mollison's only suggestion was that one or two names of members of Texas Gulf's exploration department be added. "I made no comment as to any other content of the article." The story read in part this way:

... The Northern Miner can say that something in excess of 10,000,000 tons of ore is indicated; it is capped with something like 20 ft. of overburden, presenting no stripping problems and the steep dip and wide widths will lend themselves ideally to an open-pit mining situation.

The picture should unfold rapidly at this stage, but officials emphasize that it is still at the embryo point. The company has moved with remarkable rapidity in stepping up its programs, but it is only in the past few days that it has been able to get the whole battery of drills going. And, it is a genuine fact that only limited data has been developed to the moment.

The article went on to describe the ore zone and paid tribute to Texas Gulf's exploration techniques. Near the end was this paragraph:

> The field team behind the new discovery was led by Richard D. Mollison, vice-president, exploration; Dr. Walter Holyk, chief geologist; H. V. Donohoo, chief geophysicist; Kenneth Darke, manager of the project. A number of others must also be given a share of the credit for the successful operation.

After receiving the *Northern Miner* article from Ackerley, Mollison carried it around with him for almost 24 hours. At midday on April 15, he gave the article, in a sealed envelope, to a cab driver at Toronto International Airport to be taken to the *Northern Miner* office. Mollison was a little disturbed that Ackerley had projected tonnage figures, but on the whole his reaction was, as he later said, "I wouldn't quibble with it."

The *Northern Miner* article did not appear in print until the morning of April 16, but nevertheless it had been written on April 13, the same day that the *New York Times*, the *New York Herald Tribune*, and other newspapers across the country were reporting Texas Gulf's official statement ". . . recent drilling on one property near Timmins has led to preliminary indications that more drilling would be required for proper evaluation of this prospect."

When Texas Gulf's April 12 statement appeared in the press on Monday, April 13, President Stephens began to get queries from some of his directors. A great many Texas Gulf directors, it became clear, knew nothing of the exploration work in Kidd Township, and some had never even heard of Timmins.

John Hill, the chairman of Air Reduction Company and a director of Texas Gulf, called Stephens and said, according to Stephen's recollection, "What is it all about?"

> And I said, "I don't know." We have a prospect up in Kidd Township, north of Timmins and, I said, "we are

endeavouring to get as much information as quickly as possible so that we can make a sensible announcement." I said, "The rumors have been flying in Canada because this is a very, very delicate part of the world to be working in so far as mines are concerned. It is the Porcupine area. Rumors fly quite fast up there, and furious." So, I said, "we are trying desperately to get enough information to make an announcement, if in fact we have an announcement to make."

Francis Coates, a lawyer in private practice and also a Texas Gulf director, called the same day from Houston. Coates, however, had not heard of the April 12 release; he was simply inquiring if he should come to the April 16 board meeting.

Stephens recalled, "And I said to Mr. Coates that I thought he ought to attend, if he could, because there may possibly be something to say at the board meeting because we had put out a press release."

While Mollison and Fogarty had been agonizing about the rumors printed in the New York newspapers on April 11 and 12, it was decided to bring the Ontario Minister of Mines into the picture. While it was working in Canada, Texas Gulf was not inclined to hide the fact that apart from Mollison, the four members of its metals exploration division were all Canadian citizens. From time to time Holyk had suggested, "We should have some contact with the politicians and the department of mines, and keep them abreast of what we are doing."

So, Holyk was assigned, on April 11, to get in touch with the Deputy Mines Minister, Donald Douglass, and arrange a meeting. Douglass replied that he would be with the Mines Minister, George Wardrope, in Montreal at the annual convention of the Canadian Institute of Mining and Metallurgy. It was agreed that Mollison and Holyk would fly to Montreal Tuesday, April 14, for a meeting.

George Wardrope was 70 years old, a long-time Conservative politician who reveled in making news and being the center of attention. When Mollison and Holyk arrived in Montreal on Tuesday evening, they discovered to their amazement and dismay that arrangements had been made for them to make a television announcement – the cameras and lights were in readiness.

The two Texas Gulf representatives arrived at the Queen Elizabeth Hotel between eight and nine in the evening and attempted to contact Wardrope and Douglass in their rooms. They learned that a convention banquet was in progress, so Mollison and Holyk sat down in the lobby to wait for Wardrope to emerge. Mollison tells what happened:

> While we were sitting in the lobby a chap came along that we both knew . . . it was Phil Goldsmith or something of that sort. He is with another mining company. He displayed some considerable excitement and interest when he saw us and exclaimed something to the effect, "Well, it's true. You're here."
>
> Goldsmith went on to say that many people had been waiting for the Texas Gulf men, that the TV cameras were set up, and that everybody was waiting for us to make an announcement. And my first reaction was that he was pulling our legs, but he finally convinced us he was speaking seriously.

Mollison and Holyk bolted. They took refuge in the Laurentian Hotel bar, a block or so away, from where Holyk was finally able to contact Douglass, the deputy minister, by telephone. It was arranged then that Douglass and his minister would return to Toronto at 9:30 the next morning in Texas Gulf's private plane. Mollison and Holyk spent the night at an airport hotel. Unknown to them, that same evening at the Queen Elizabeth Hotel, Viola MacMillan, Canada's first lady of mining, was holding a reception in her suite. Viola was whispering to some of her guests what purported to be the assay results from hole K-55-1. According to one of those guests, her figures were remarkably close, if not exact.

Flying back to Toronto with Wardrope and Douglass was for Mollison and Holyk an opportunity to brief them on the results of exploration at Kidd 55. Nothing more was intended, but Wardrope's anxiety to make a public statement was such that he was able to wrest from Mollison a written statement by the time the plane arrived in Toronto 90 minutes later.

Holyk sat with Douglass on one side of the small plane. He unfolded a map and read to Douglass composite assays of the first drill hole. Over the noise of the engines, Holyk could hear only snatches of the conversation between Mollison and Wardrope.

Wardrope had a busy day ahead. He was due at the legislative buildings during the afternoon, and was scheduled to make a dinner speech at a town 60 miles west of Toronto. After conferring with Douglass, Wardrope decided he could be back in Toronto in time to make a statement on the 11 o'clock national television news. That, at least, was the plan as it was represented to Mollison.

According to Mollison, Wardrope had also told him that in the absence of a statement from the Mines Minister, the three Toronto daily newspapers would be at his throat. It was important, he argued, that he not appear ignorant of the discovery. Mollison's concern was that the New York press not be scooped. It may have been that in allowing the 11 p.m. release he was unaware of the breadth of the Canadian viewing public. The 11 o'clock national news on the publicly owned Canadian Broadcasting Corporation network is an institution in Canada; it has an audience of several million viewers.

Wardrope's own recollection of the plane trip differed slightly but significantly from Mollison's. A statement made by Wardrope concerning the trip did not indicate the release was prepared at his behest. Rather, it implied that Mollison had volunteered the releases; "Mr. Mollison gave us a statement and asked that it not be released before 11 p.m. that evening."

Following this lengthy discussion, Mollison took from his pocket some stationery bearing the letterhead, "Bon Air Motor Hotel." He wrote out a statement, made some corrections, and rewrote it on another sheet of paper. One copy he gave to Wardrope.

The statement was not given on the 11 o'clock news by Wardrope. It was not issued until, in a slightly different form, it was distributed to members of the press gallery in the provincial legislature the next morning, April 16, at 9:40. Wardrope, with typically unrestrained enthusiasm, calculated that he would not be able to return to Toronto by 11 o'clock. So he had his public relations director prepare the statement on the afternoon of the 15th, and gave no instructions for an embargo. Had it not been for Douglass's intervention, the Mollison statement would have gone to the newspapers at midafternoon on April 15.

This was the release that was finally issued by the office of the Mines Minister. Inexplicably, it was dated April 16, and asserted that the statement from Mollison was received on the morning of that date:

The following report has been received this morning from R. D. Mollison, vice president – exploration, Texas Gulf Sulphur Company:

There have been rumors during the past few weeks about the exploration work of Texas Gulf Sulphur Company north of Timmins, Ontario, in Kidd township. Until only 10 days ago TGS had only one diamond drill operating and there really was no basis for the rumors. A second machine began operating on April 6, but only part time because extremely cold weather restricted the amount of water available for drilling. With the warmer weather of the past week, water was more easily found, so that a third drill was started on April 10, and a fourth on April 12. This intensification of work in the last few days has resulted in a rapid accumulation of significantly more data than the company had as recently as this past weekend.

There are still only six drill holes complete enough to be important in evaluating the sulphide body being explored, and actual assays from only one hole, but the information now in hand from this limited work gives the company confidence to allow me to announce that Texas Gulf Sulphur has a mineable body of zinc, copper, silver ore of substantial dimensions that will be developed and brought to production as rapidly as possible.

When Mollison and Holyk and their two guests arrived at Toronto International Airport, Mollison promptly phoned Fogarty in New York and recounted his discussions with Wardrope. Fogarty expressed no objection when he learned a statement had been given to the Mines Minister.

Texas Gulf's two senior exploration men said goodbye to Wardrope and Douglass and boarded a plane for Timmins and one last inspection before the next day's board meeting. After a quick visit to the property and a short briefing from Ken Darke, Mollison and Holyk returned to New York, taking with them drill logs and several boxes of core from K-55-3. They were back in New York before 10 o'clock, where they were met at the airport by John Murray, office manager for Texas Gulf. With Murray, they drove to the company's Park Avenue offices, where busy preparations were being made for the board meeting and the first official announcement – in the United States – of the discovery.

Chapter Fifteen

THE MEETING

David Crawford didn't arrive at the Texas Gulf office any too early on the morning of Thursday, April 16. He had arrived back from his familiarization trip to Houston only the day before, and he'd spent the night at the Drake Hotel. Crawford had joined Texas Gulf in January that year, and although he was the director of government and public relations as well as the secretary, he had known nothing about the Kidd Township exploration until a few days before.

On his way to Houston, he had stopped off at Chicago, where he had been employed by Abbott Laboratories, to attempt to sell or rent his house there. He had arrived in Houston early Sunday evening, and met Harold Kline, Texas Gulf's general counsel, in the company's suite at the Shamrock

Hilton Hotel. There was some discussion about the rumors that had appeared in the New York newspapers of April 11, and Kline mentioned that Texas Gulf officials in New York might be preparing a release of some sort.

The April 12 release, the one describing the Kidd-55 property as a "prospect" that needed further evaluation, was first seen by Crawford as it came over the Telex in Texas Gulf's Houston office.

Upon his Wednesday arrival in the New York office, Executive Vice-president Charles Fogarty told Crawford to stay within earshot because there was going to be a press conference the next day. During the afternoon Fogarty again called Crawford into his office, and handed him a copy of Mollison's written statement to Wardrope. Crawford was first to communicate the contents of this release to Texas Gulf's regional managers in North America, and then he was to invite members of the press to a conference in Texas Gulf's office the next morning at 10 o'clock. Once those duties were discharged, Crawford was recruited into the team that was to draft the announcement for the next day's press conference.

"I would say that from late afternoon until it [the announcement] was put into final form I was in and out of his [Fogarty's] office almost constantly. It would have been from approximately 4:30 or 5 until somewhere around 11 o'clock that night."

In the preparation of the announcement, Fogarty and Crawford were assisted by a Mr. Orlando of the public relations firm, Doremus and Company; President Claude Stephens was present from time to time, and on one of these occasions mentioned that the Minister of Mines for Ontario was making a statement on television in Canada that night.

The Texas Gulf anouncement was to a great extent based on the contents of the Wardrope statement, Crawford said later. This statement, and information he was given verbally by Fogarty, was the full extent of his knowledge about the status of exploration at Kidd-55. Crawford was not shown any logs, maps or other data which, in any case, would have meant little to him since his background was not in mining.

With the public relations man, Orlando, he had the Texas Gulf announcement typed and retyped until it was ready for distribution. It was about midnight, and Crawford was one of the last to leave Texas Gulf's offices that night. He called his wife in Vernon, New Jersey, to tell her he wouldn't be home, and went over to the company's suite in the Park Lane Hotel to spend the night. From there he called a friend in Chicago, Edward Hurd, a stockbroker. "Buy me 300 shares of Texas Gulf at the market," he said. To this time, Crawford had never owned a share of Texas Gulf. In the past he'd owned such stocks as Socony Vacuum, Allied Chemical, RCA, Eastman Kodak, and Bristol Myers, and the gross value of his holdings was between $20,000 and $25,000.

"He [Hurd] probably asked me how my family was, and I asked him how his family was." Crawford was tired, and he didn't remember much more of that conversation, except that he had told Hurd he had some shares pledged with a trust company which could be used as credit against the purchase of Texas Gulf shares. (Later, Crawford borrowed $4,000 from the First National City Bank to pay for the Texas Gulf shares.)

Crawford awoke before eight the next morning, and upon further brief contemplation decided to call Hurd again and increase his order from 300 shares to 600 shares. The Chicago broker entered orders for the account of Mr. and Mrs. Crawford at 8:48 a.m. and 8:49 a.m. Chicago time (an hour later New York time), and the transactions were executed at a price of $30.12 as to 500 shares and $30.25 as to 100 shares.

Francis G. Coates, a Houston lawyer and a member of the firm of Baker, Botts, Shepherd and Coates, had been on the

Texas Gulf board of directors since 1949. He had never heard of Timmins until Monday, April 13, 1964, when he called Claude Stephens from Houston to ask if he needed to attend the April 16 board meeting.

> He [Stephens] asked me whether I had read in any newspaper about Timmins and I told him I had not, and he referred me to the *Wall Street Journal,* and I got that and read the article. He didn't tell me very much more. He said what we were thinking about: If further information obtained by exploration justified it, making a public announcement of the results of the activity near Timmins.

Stephens told Coates to be sure to attend the directors' meeting.

With his wife, Coates flew to New York Wednesday, April 15. He said later that it was during that plane journey that he determined to buy more shares of Texas Gulf.

After checking into a hotel and doing an errand or two, Coates dropped in at the Texas Gulf office about four o'clock

> About the time I got there, there was brought into Mr. Stephens what looked like a very rough and early draft of an announcement of the discovery near Timmins as being a major discovery. Stephens showed it to me. I read the first two or three lines and he said, "Well, you will learn about it tomorrow."

Coates could see that Stephens was busy, and he stayed only a few minutes.

Thomas Lamont had joined the board of Texas Gulf in November of 1927, the heyday of Walter Aldridge, and although he had retired from the Morgan Guaranty Trust Company in January, 1964, he remained as Texas Gulf's senior director. Lamont had a wide variety of business interests, and in latter years he had traveled around the country to inspect the businesses of companies whose boards he graced. He had become a kind of liaison man between these companies and Morgan Guaranty. It had been Lamont, with his breadth of experience, whom Stephens had come to for advice about the discovery rumors the previous week.

After that conversation with Stephens, Lamont saw reports of the April 12 press release in New York newspapers the next day. He had a number of casual conversations in the next day, "just generally . . . with friends, people I would run into." One of these conversations was with Longstreet Hinton, a close personal friend, who was executive vice-president of Morgan Guaranty Trust Company, the head of its 400-person trust and investment department, and the man with unchallenged authority to buy securities on Morgan Guaranty's behalf.

Lamont had over a period of a few years suggested to Hinton that Texas Gulf might be a worthwhile purchase for the various accounts administered by the trust company. As far as he knew, Hinton had not acted on his recommendation. But when the April 12 release was made public, Hinton telephoned Lamont.

> The brief substance of my conversation with Hinton would be that I would have met him in the hall or at lunch or something and he might have telephoned, and he in brief said that he had seen all these stories and did I know anything about them. And I said I knew no more than what had appeared in the press.

On April 15, Stephens called Lamont to tell him to be sure to attend the next day's board meeting. Stephens mentioned also that there would be a press conference following the board meeting, but Lamont remembered nothing about being told the subject of the press conference.

The meeting began promptly at nine o'clock; all 15 directors were present. It was tradition at Texas Gulf to hold board meetings on the third Thursday of each month. This meeting was in the windowless board room of the company's new offices in the Pan Am building, across the hall from the offices of Stephens and Fogarty.

The decision to allow the board meeting to meld, as it were, into the press conference, was not made until the afternoon of the day before. It was a decision reached by Stephens and Fogarty. Fogarty said afterwards:

> We were just quite concerned during this period of time and under quite a pressure and responsibility, and we felt that by having a press conference – I called a press conference late in the afternoon of Wednesday, the 15th, and the subconscious idea, I suppose, was that this was the best medium to get maximum coverage to everyone at the same time.

The vague nature of the April 12 release had led to varied interpretations in the newspapers, and some editorial comment, which "alarmed" Fogarty, "plus the fact that we were getting more and more questions being asked by everybody, because now that the April 12 release was disseminated to the public, this now caused everyone to ask questions, what does it mean, and so forth. . . ."

The first 15 to 20 minutes of the board meeting was spent going over the minutes of the last meeting, and reviewing routine reports on the progress of the company. Then there were some spending appropriations of a size which required board approval. Finally, Stephens said he wanted to talk about Kidd-55. The board was not accustomed to dealing with matters having to do with metals exploration. Drilling for sulphur, or even oil, was frequently brought to their attention, in part because of the large costs associated with drilling oil or sulphur wells. It was also a fact that the company's history and tradition was in the field of sulphur, and this was what most directors were familiar with, and interested in.

Coates, the Houston lawyer, was the first to ask a question:

I asked him [Stephens] whether he was reasonably sure that he did have a major discovery, because I was apprehensive lest we would announce a major discovery and then it would pinch out, as they say in the mining world, and then we would be in a very bad odor in Canada. There was quite full attendance and everybody had questions; we did very little at the meeting except approve the minutes of the prior meeting, and the main order of business was Timmins.

That morning in New York City, 1,412 subscribers received their copies of the *Northern Miner* and were able to read a story with the headline, "Texas Gulf Sulphur Comes Up with Major Find Carrying Important Copper, Zinc, Silver Values." There is no evidence as to what time the *Miner* reached newsstands. In the investment community it didn't matter: when the *Northern Miner* became available in Toronto at eight a.m., the wires between Toronto and New York were hot with reports of the story.

While the board meeting was going on, Orlando, the public relations man, was shepherding 22 members of the press into Texas Gulf's reception area. Some time before 10:30, the reporters were ushered into the board room. Among them were a representative of Dow Jones News Service, purveyors of the broad tape, and Norma Walter, who was accredited by *Investor's Reader*, a publication of Merrill Lynch, Pierce, Fenner and Smith.

Stephens had invited the directors to remain through the press conference, and all did, at least at the beginning. He and Fogarty introduced themselves to the reporters, distributed copies of the announcement, and began to read from it. Some of those present didn't wait to hear the oratory; they left the room immediately in search of the nearest telephone. This was the announcement:

Texas Gulf Sulphur Company has made a major strike of zinc, copper and silver in the Timmins area of Ontario, Canada. . . .

Seven drill holes are now essentially complete and indicate an ore body of at least 800 feet in length, 300 feet in width and having a vertical depth of more than 800 feet. . . .

This is a major discovery. The preliminary data indicate a reserve of more than 25 million tons of ore. The only hole assayed so far represents over 600 feet of ore, indicating a true thickness of nearly 400 feet. . . .

Visual examination of cores from the other holes indicates comparable grade and continuity of ore.

The ore body is shallow, having only some 20 feet of overburden. This means that it can easily be mined initially by the open pit method.

Stephens had barely read the first sentence before some reporters left the room. Two of the earliest to leave were Norma Walter, the Merrill Lynch representative, and the reporter for Dow Jones News Service.

The first one to reach a phone was Jerry Bishop, a *Wall Street Journal* reporter, who transmitted his story in three separate "takes" so that the essence of the news – confirmation of the discovery – would get on the wire as instantly as possible. But for some reason which has never been explained, it was 45 minutes before Bishop's report appeared on the D-J ticker at 10:45 a.m. The two subsequent takes were transmitted at intervals to 11:02 o'clock. This peculiar delay (normally, news of much less significance is on the tape within a few minutes) became an important part of the case against one of the Texas Gulf insiders. Norma Walter of Merrill Lynch reached the telephone shortly afterwards. A summary of her report went on the big brokerage firm's internal teletype network at 10:29 a.m. and was carried into several hundred Merrill Lynch offices.

Despite their diminishing audience, Stephens and Fogarty went through the remaining motions of the press conference, ultimately putting on display five or six colored slides of the Timmins discovery site.

They weren't very inspiring slides, as Coates, the director, later recalled:

> There was snow and cold-looking men dressed in warm working clothes, and a core-drilling rig, and that was about all. I can't recall any questions asked Mr. Stephens at that time. Most of them [the reporters] seemed to be anxious to get out and get their stories back to their respective publications.

What was left of the assembly adjourned to an adjoining room, where samples of the wide-diameter mill core were on display.

Coates stayed only three or four minutes, before strolling across the hall to Claude Stephen's office. He telephoned the switchboard of his Houston law firm and asked to be connected with Raucher, Pierce and Company, a brokerage firm where his son-in-law, Fred Haemissegger, worked. The fact that he routed his telephone call this way indicated the sense of urgency Coates felt. "I did it this way because the headquarters of Raucher, Pierce is in Dallas, they don't have many trunk lines into their Houston office, and I wanted to reach Mr. Haemissegger promptly."

Coates, who had not bought Texas Gulf shares since August, 1963, instructed his son-in-law to place an order for

500 shares for each of the four Coates family trusts at a price not to exceed $32. Haemissegger executed the order at prices between $31 and $31.62, and thereupon passed the news of the discovery to four of his customers. The customers, and Haemissegger himself, bought a total of 1,500 shares at prices from $31.25 to $35.

Coates had telephoned his son-in-law shortly before 10:20 a.m., at least 34 minutes before the discovery news first passed over the Dow Jones broad tape. He later excused his actions by saying, "I relied on that news service to function as I had been observing it to function in all the years I had been on the board: When we put out a dividend announcement, that usually it gets on the broad tape in two to four minutes."

Following the press conference, Thomas Lamont moved into the adjoining room to view the samples of core. "I listened to some of them chatter and talk with each other, and slapped people on the back." At 10:40 he used a nearby telephone to call Longstreet Hinton at Morgan Guaranty Trust, and said that an announcement would shortly be coming over the Dow Jones ticker.

Hinton asked "Is it good?" and Lamont's recollection is that he replied either, "Sure, pretty good," or "Very good." Hinton was no more than a few strides from the Dow Jones machine in his office, but his first move was to call his stock trading department and ask about the market action of Texas Gulf shares. He was told that the stock was active, and selling for $3 more than the closing price the previous day. Hinton instructed that 2,000 shares be purchased for the Nassau Hospital Association, of which he was treasurer and trustee. Thereafter, Hinton gave instructions for the purchase of a total 10,000 shares for customers of Morgan Guaranty, and the stock was bought for prices between $32.62 and $34.

At the sec's offices in Washington, Ingrid Nelson was at her usual post in the ticker room amid the chatter of stock market tapes and the Dow Jones news service machine – the broad tape. In this room the commission monitors stock price changes and compares unusual trading activity to news passing over the broad tape. When Miss Nelson, an SEC financial analyst, saw the first few words of the Texas Gulf announcement – and then the phrase, "major discovery," she penciled on the broad tape, "April 16, 1055."

For several days Miss Nelson had been watching the symbol TG pass more frequently on the New York Stock Exchange ticker tape, accompanied by a rising price. "I thought the commission might be interested in this release...remembering that the statement of Monday had said the rumors were exaggerated and that there had been no find."

Around noontime, Lamont went by car to his downtown office which was in the same building as Morgan Guaranty Trust at 15 Broad Street. A few minutes after arriving, he ordered 3,000 Texas Gulf shares for himself and members of his family. The order was executed at a price of $34.50 – at 12:33 p.m.

By any previous standards, Lamont's personal acquisition of Texas Gulf shares would have been free of the suggestion of insider exploitation. It happened almost two hours after the news went across the Dow Jones broad tape. But the Securities and Exchange Commission, in an attempt to broaden the interpretation of insider trading laws, said later:

> The commission does not contend that the information containing Texas Gulf's drilling results in Kidd township was reported to the public at any precise moment.
>
> It contends that this information was reported to the public by means of a continuing process of reporting and dissemination of news involving various news media, including wire services, newspapers of general circulation, financial newspapers and other financial publica-

tions, which process commenced in the United States following the meeting with reporters . . . and which process continued for several days thereafter.

It is the commission's position that even after corporate information has been published in the news media, insiders still are under a duty to refrain from securities transactions until there has elapsed a reasonable amount of time in which the securities industry, the shareholders and the investing public can evaluate the development and make informed investment decisions.

Chapter Sixteen

THE PENNY STOCK HYSTERIA

Less than one month before Texas Gulf Sulphur Company announced its Kidd Creek discovery, the Toronto Stock Exchange lost all hope for a company called Glenn Uranium Mines Ltd. and suspended the company's shares from trading privileges. Glenn shares had been languishing at four-and-a-half cents each, a value that accrued to them only by virtue of the fact that the company had a listing on the stock exchange. Glenn had no fixed assets, and its most prominent liquid asset was a $5,000 note receivable which was more than three years overdue. Its debts, on the other hand, were enough to smother a much larger and healthier corporation; creditors were lined up to the tune of $335,000, and there was little prospect of ever satisfying them. Glenn Uranium Mines might have passed into history there and then had it not been for the discovery by Texas Gulf Sulphur. Instead it became one of the most sought-after speculative stocks on the Toronto exchange; in a matter of weeks the public poured $260,000 into its treasury – and much more into the pockets of its promoters.

Glenn Uranium Mines became one of the star performers in the maddest scramble that has ever taken place on any stock exchange. Along with a dozen or so other companies which bought ground near the Texas Gulf strike, it turned the Toronto stock market into such a frenzy of activity that companies were actually requested to issue new treasury shares to accommodate public demand which otherwise would have driven the price of some stocks to even more unrealistic levels. The target of speculators was anything that moved in the Timmins area.

The cautionary tone of Texas Gulf's April 12 press release ("drilling done to date has not been conclusive") was not reflected in trading the next day on the Toronto Stock Exchange. More than 4,500,000 shares changed hands in the first hour of trading, a record even for Toronto's penny casino. That was only the beginning, however.

Texas Gulf's second press release issued April 16 ("Texas Gulf Sulphur has a mineable body of zinc, copper, and silver ore of substantial dimensions") was followed by a record-shattering volume of 28,704,000 shares. One company alone, Central Porcupine Mines, traded more than 5,386,000 shares after picking up a property near Timmins. Significantly, the average price of each share that changed hands that day was a lowly 40¢ – even though the majority of companies listed on the Toronto Stock Exchange are industrial and productive resource companies whose shares sell at much higher prices.

Board rooms of brokerage firms, which normally resemble funeral parlors, were clogged and noisy with customers and sightseers. The ticker tape ran as much as 45 minutes late, and the Toronto Stock Exchange computer was, on one occasion, millions of shares in error in its calculation of total volume. Stockbrokers had their clerical staffs working until midnight, and it was common practice to double salaries in return for this extra duty.

Glenn Uranium Mines, meanwhile, was reinstated by the Toronto Stock Exchange and almost immediately began trading at 50¢ – a 1,150% appreciation from its 4¢ price of a month before when the trading suspension was brought down. Glenn eventually rose to 85¢, but like all the other penny dreadfuls it had only a fleeting moment of glory: A year later the stock was 11¢.

How Glenn won its way back into grace at the stock exchange, and how it enticed the public to buy millions of its shares, is the best illustration of the mania that was focused on Timmins. Twenty-eight-year-old Pasquale Giardine, previously described in connection with Bunker Hill, arranged to buy control of the company and simultaneously arranged for the payment of its creditors at a rate of 20¢ on the dollar. On April 14, Glenn agreed to buy four mining claims at a location four miles distant from the Texas Gulf discovery. Since the company had no money to pay for these claims, nor to make a settlement with its creditors, Giardine arranged for the sale of one million Glenn shares to the public at prices between 20¢ and 35¢. For the mining claims, Glenn paid $20,000 and 400,000 of its own newly issued shares.

In order to get approval for this series of transactions, Giardine had to show the Toronto Stock Exchange that the mining claims held promise of some value. After all, they would be the company's only asset, and it was on the basis of these claims alone that the public was being offered one million shares. (Actually this was only the publicly announced policy of the stock exchange; in actual fact, the exchange didn't even make preliminary inquiries as to whether Glenn could get title to the claims.)

To establish the potential value of the claims, Giardine retained the services of a geologist. The geologist's report, circulated among the public, neatly sidestepped the important fact that no exploration work had been done on the claims. The report included these comments:

The four unpatented mining claims described in this report are located in an area where high-grade copper has been unofficially reported in diamond drilling. The rocks of the area may be considered as favorable for possible mineral deposits. . . .

The claims are approximately 15 miles north-north-east of Timmins, Ontario, and are not presently accessible by road. In summer, the only easy access may be by helicopter.

The claims were staked recently, following rumors of a copper strike nearby.

Due to general lack of rock outcrop and present heavy snow cover, no personal examination has been possible. . . .

A recently published map of the Ontario Department of Mines indicates a probable sediment-lava contact just south of the claim group. From experience to date, the sediments are not favorable for base metal (i.e. copper) deposition and exploration should be confined to the contact zone and the lavas to the north.

The area is one of great interest because of the copper discovery which has been unofficially reported. The discovery is reported in drilling three miles west-southwest of the claims and is said to have been made as a result of airborne electromagnetic surveys.

The geologist recommended a program of preliminary surface exploration which could be completed within 10 days at a cost of less than $4,000.

It was on the basis of this document that the public was being asked to buy one million shares of Glenn Uranium. But first a private company owned by Glenn's president, Giardine, bought the shares directly from the treasury for a total price of $260,000. For these same shares, the public paid Giardine's company $591,166.

Ken Darke was one of the few people to make money in Glen Uranium. He was aware that the claims were of little value and sold the stock short. He made $6,905.40.

One year later, Giardine reported to the shareholders of Glenn Uranium Mines that two drill holes on the four claims had intersected "no mineralization of economic interest," but by now the market play was over and no one seemed to care.

Not only small mining promoters were involved in these underwritings. Perhaps the busiest investment firm in Canada in mid-April, 1964, was Doherty, Roadhouse and McCuaig Brothers, one of the country's biggest brokers and specialists in mining stocks. Doherty-Roadhouse owned three memberships on the Toronto Stock Exchange, and therefore was entitled to 15 floor traders. It was estimated that Doherty-Roadhouse was responsible for 10% of the trading volume on the exchange.

Some of the partners of Doherty-Roadhouse had other interests, as well as acting in their most apparent role as agents for the public. Four of its partners were directors of an investor-owned corporation called PCE Explorations Limited. The only other director of PCE was Murray Watts, the president of a firm of mining engineering consultants. Early in April, PCE bought a group of 12 Timmins-area mining claims from a private company called Mine Securities Ltd. for $73,000 cash and 200,000 PCE shares. The officers and directors of Mine Securities Ltd. were all partners of Doherty-

Roadhouse. Mine Securities had purchased the claims from Nedo Bragagnolo the day before. (Later Walter Holyk said that these claims were of no interest and had no reasonable chance of containing an ore body).

The geologist's report necessary to get stock exchange approval for the acquisition of the claims was written by Murray Watts, the director of PCE.

Contemporaneous with the purchase of the claims, PCE sought and won stock exchange approval to sell one million newly issued treasury shares. Doherty-Roadhouse handled the public distribution of this stock, acting on behalf of Murray Watts and Speculative Investments Limited. One of the directors of Speculative Investments was a partner of Murray Watts in his mining engineering firm.

The Toronto Stock Exchange did not give its blessing to this series of transactions until April 10. Nevertheless, in the two days preceding, Doherty-Roadhouse sold to the public 802,000 of the million treasury shares – shares which had yet to be issued from the treasury and, therefore, for all legal purposes did not exist!

By the time the million shares were distributed to the public, the treasury of PCE was richer by $335,000 and the underwriters, Speculative Investments Limited and Murray Watts, had profited by $122,000. There was no way to estimate the commission profit made by Doherty, Roadhouse and company.

The system whereby private individuals and companies bought treasury shares at fixed, negotiated prices and then resold them to the public at whatever the market would bear had two effects: It was to the promoter's advantage to get the market price of the stock as high as possible to maximize his profits; the public, aware of the promoter's position, encouraged the chances of his success by hurrying to capitalize on any rise in price the promoter might be able to induce. Each individual hoped to sell out before the inevitable collapse. The catalyst was always the prospect of drill-hole news, and the gambling instinct was always most urgent before drill-hole results – good or bad – were announced. PCE Explorations, like other companies whose fortunes were tied to Timmins-area drilling activity, fell into this pattern. The stock rose from 10¢ to $1.25, but within little more than a year it was back to 16¢.

The record-breaking trading volume of Friday, April 17, brought an extraordinary statement of caution from the president of the Toronto Stock Exchange, Howard Graham, who made the superfluous observation that some members of the public were bound to lose money. Unfortunately, this was followed by a report in the press quoting Mr. George Hees, the new president of the Montreal and Canadian Stock Exchanges, that, "The speculative boom is soundly based." The Montreal Exchange became aware that some of the hot penny stocks were now trading for more than one dollar and therefore qualified for margin privileges. The Montreal Exchange quite properly threatened to suspend margin buying for stocks of this type. It didn't, however, and the professional investment community had good reasons of self-interest for not doing so. Brokerage commissions were running at as much as $700,000 per day, a figure which in more serene times would take a week or more to accumulate.

Canadian mining promoters were all so anxious to cut themselves into these windfall profits that they rushed by the hundreds to Timmins in an effort to buy land near the Texas Gulf discovery. One promoter was in such a hurry that he even advertised that his company had purchased claims that it did not own. Steven Low, in his capacity as president of Bruce-Presto Mines Ltd. (whose shares were underwritten by Tuina Enterprises Ltd. – president, Steven Low), made on a Friday an oral deal with a prospector in Timmins to acquire for his company a group of claims, and on the same day sent off the money to pay for them. That same day he also gave orders for the insertion in Monday's *Globe and Mail* of a flamboyant advertisement stating that the company had acquired those claims. The advertisement appeared on the Monday, and on the Tuesday Mr. Low was informed that the deal had fallen through because the prospector had reneged. Later Mr. Low explained to the Securities Commission that, "This could happen to anybody."

The Timmins' spree defied comparison with any of history's other excesses on the Toronto Stock Exchange. The big trading volumes began after World War II, when broad public participation in the market commenced. The first splurge started on August 31, 1949, when newspapers reported "wave after wave" of buying aimed at shares of companies holding gold prospects in the Larder Lake area of Ontario. Trading volume that day was 2,500,000 shares. The Korean War touched off a rise in world prices for zinc, lead, and copper, and that was the start of the rootin' tootin' markets of the 1950s. On January 15, 1953, a record 6,400,000 shares changed hands. Within weeks a base metals find in New Brunswick and uranium exploration in northern Saskatchewan helped to generate a new trading volume of 12,246,000 shares. In 1955, with uranium fever spreading down from Blind River on the northern rim of Lake Huron, it was not uncommon for low-priced mining and oil stocks to account for 98% of trading on the Toronto market. Finally, in July, 1958, the great copper discovery in the Mattagami area of Quebec drove trading volume on one day to 15,800,000 shares. That record stood until Timmins.

What was characteristic of all these stock market orgies was the lack of interest on the part of the public in buying shares of a successful mine. A study prepared for the Royal Commission on Banking and Finance came to the statistical and sad conclusion that the shares of a mining exploration company usually decline if the company finds a mine. At first, the study reported, "the public is gambling largely on selling the stock at a quick profit, and so the market becomes a kind of lottery on each drill hole." Once a mine is found, the long risk, the unknown element, are removed; even though the shares may be substantially enhanced in real value because of the discovery, the public loses interest. Some of the biggest – and surest – stock market profits have been made by people who buy shares during this post-discovery depression.

Brunswick Mining and Smelting Corporation is a typical example. This company was formed in October, 1952, to explore a lead-zinc property in New Brunswick. When diamond drilling that year and the next indicated a large base metals orebody, Brunswick shares shot to $23.75. There was no question that this was a rich mine which would sooner or later be put into production, but the speculators were impatient. The stock fell to as low as $1.95 in 1958, and it never again reached $23.75. It did, however, climb quickly in 1964 – from $6.25 to $16.75 – when money from Belgian financiers finally allowed Brunswick to begin extracting ore.

The Northgate Explorations example is even more striking. This company had been an active exploration company in the late 1950s under the direction of its president, Irish-born stock promoter Patrick Hughes. When the Canadian company began to explore a lead-zinc prospect in late 1961, Northgate's shares were 38¢. The first drill hole returned high lead values, and the stock rose to $1.46. Assay results from the second hole early in January, 1962, sent the stock higher by $1.23 in one day. As each succeeding drill hole increased the known dimensions of the orebody, Northgate shares rose until they reached a high of $8.55 in 1962.

Then, after 47 drill holes had established that Northgate had a rich producing mine on its hands, the speculators sold the company's shares. Within a year the stock was $2.80. It took three years to get back to the $8.55 level of 1962 when it had not yet been certain that Northgate had found a commercial orebody. Eventually, when full-scale production got under way, Northgate climbed above $18 per share.

The Timmins phenomenon may be the last concentrated blast of stock market speculation based on low-priced resource exploration stocks in Canada. For one thing, the discovery of new mines is now largely in the hands of big corporations, using sophisticated survey techniques such as those employed by Texas Gulf Sulphur. For another, no matter how much the public may be willing to be taken for a ride by the stock promoters, government is slowly removing the incentive to the promoters with laws designed to prevent the money of public speculators from being diverted into the pockets of promoters.

The study for the Royal Commission on Banking and Finance calculated that new mine exploration financing through the sale to the public of penny stocks totalled $340 million between 1953 and 1960. Of this amount, only $150 million was actually spent for exploration. The $340 million, of course, is simply the cash that went into company treasuries; it may bear no resemblance to the total amount of money contributed by the public, much of which goes to stock promoters.

It is estimated that out of every dollar that the public spends on penny stocks less than 20¢ actually goes toward exploration.

Because the Timmins spree had given an unpleasant odor to the whole mining industry, the Ontario government undertook a survey to determine the motives of penny stock speculators. It found that more than half the speculators realized they were taking an outright gamble. But as the study noted, it is disturbing that even a large minority should believe otherwise.

The one outstanding and amazing fact is that the whole Timmins penny stock boom was predicated on the purchase and drilling of lands which were entirely valueless and which Texas Gulf Sulphur had already examined and discarded. Yet the promoters rushed to buy this worthless moose pasture and to sell it at vastly inflated prices to the gullible public – and the government did nothing.

Here is the sad 1964 story of some of the 61 other small mining exploration companies listed on the Toronto Stock Exchange which held properties near Timmins:

	1964 low	Height of hysteria	End of 1964
Belleterre Quebec Mines	21	84	47
Bibis Yukon Mines	20	33	23
Cam Mines	17½	52	25
Candore Explorations	11	64	13½
Central Porcupine Mines	6	25	17
Chesterville Mines	13	32½	16
Genex Mines	9½	61	24
Goldfields Mining	15½	86	41
Kirkland Minerals	13	49½	15
North Rankin Nickel Mines	24	54	33
Salem Exploration	21	70	25
Silver-Miller Mines	15	22	17

What chance did individual speculators have to sell out before the collapse? The investigating commission discovered that 85% of the stockholders still held their deflated stock one year later and that only half of those who had sold out had got out at a profit. In other words, 92% of the investing public lost their money.

Chapter Seventeen

THE LEITCH SIDESHOW

Suddenly Texas Gulf's ownership of the $2 billion orebody was challenged by one man.

The man who founded Leitch Gold Mines may be one of the last pick-and-shovel prospectors to make millions out of mining. Karl Springer is not a man given to old-fashioned ideas, but he gives lie to the belief that the discovery of mineral deposits can only be made by large corporations such as Texas Gulf Sulphur Company who use sophisticated, expensive techniques to find wealth hidden beneath the ground. For four and a half years, Springer threatened to wrest from Texas Gulf its newly discovered Kidd Creek mine; the chances of his winning may have been small, but they were appealing enough that intelligent stock market speculators were willing to risk as much as $75 million that he would win.

Springer was 65 years old when Texas Gulf announced on April 16, 1964, that it had found an orebody of massive proportions in Kidd Township, 14 miles north of Timmins. The revelation was far more interesting to Springer than to most people, because his Leitch Gold Mines had one year before entered into an exploration agreement which gave it rights to lands tantalizingly close to the Kidd 55 site. In Springer's view the agreement covered the lands which contained the huge orebody. He may very well have been correct.

Springer's formal education ended in public school. He took night school classes in geology and mineralogy, and began his mining career in the wild Rouyn camp in the early 1920s. After prospecting all over northern Ontario and northern Quebec, he formed, in 1935, Leitch Gold Mines to develop a gold prospect near Beardmore, Ontario. Springer was then 35 years old. Over the next quarter century the Beardmore property produced more than $24 million of gold bullion.

That was just the beginning for Karl Springer. He was an advocate of small prospecting syndicates, and it was a system that worked well.

In 1944 he founded Canadian Industrial Minerals Ltd., a barite producer in Nova Scotia which went on to be the source of $44 million of ore. Two years later he put together a group of small silver producers at the other end of the country and formed Mastodon-Highland Bell Mines Ltd., one of Canada's major silver producers. In those same years he bought a small bush aircraft operation, Central British Columbia Airways, and eventually turned it into Canada's third-largest airline, Pacific Western Airlines.

Springer's aviation interests led to the formation of Helicopter Explorations in 1950. This was one of the first companies to use helicopters for aerial exploration; its aircraft helped to find the Granduc copper mine in British Columbia.

But Karl Springer's achievements were to become even greater in his later years, for in 1956, he formed the Mattagami Syndicate which discovered the vast, multi-mineral Mattagami Lake Mines. And within the next two years he had organized the Mackenzie Syndicate, whose work led to the formation of Canada Tungsten Mining Corporation. This mine in the Northwest Territories is the third-largest tungsten producer in the world.

Barely was the ink dry on Texas Gulf's discovery announcement when Leitch shares began to bubble on the stock market. The company's Beardmore property was about to run out of gold ore, and its shares had sagged to as low as $1.30 in 1963. By the time of the Texas Gulf announcement, Leitch stock had recovered to $2.15.

There now occurred an episode which illustrated perfectly the inadequacy of Canadian mining laws. International Mining Corporation of New York had been acquiring Leitch shares on a straight investment basis for the previous three years. They now held slightly over 500,000 shares. On May 4, 1964, Fred E. Hall, Executive Vice-president of Leitch, approached International Mining and offered "on behalf of a group" to purchase International Mining's entire 500,000 shares at a price of $2.30 a share. Fortunately for them the executives of International Mining were suspicious and did not accept the offer; it was allowed to lapse on May 8. Two weeks later their stock had increased in value by over a million dollars.

When he was asked by a reporter in May of 1969 about the 1964 offer for the 500,000 Leitch shares, Hall said, "I'd forget it. What's the point in bringing up all that stuff?"

He refused to identify members of the group he had acted for, and added that his motive had been, "trying to keep control of the company in Canada."

Hall said that International Mining Corporation had been steadily acquiring shares of Leitch and "tried to push their way into the company." He said that after he wrote to International Mining with the offer to buy 500,000 shares, International Mining turned his letter over to Texas Gulf and told Texas Gulf that Hall was engaged in a "market play." In any event, Hall said, his offer was made "before anything on Texas Gulf" – meaning that Leitch was not yet contemplating a lawsuit against Texas Gulf.

During the remainder of May, more than two million shares changed hands, and the price of Leitch rose to as high as $4.80. Directors of the company – those who could be reached – refused to make any clarifying statement.

Leitch and a subsidiary company, Mastodon-Highland Bell Mines Ltd. filed their writ on June 5, 1964, seven weeks after the disclosure of Texas Gulf's Kidd Township discovery. Leitch quickly rose to $7.50; Highland Bell was $9, up from $3 only weeks before.

Texas Gulf Sulphur's president, Claude Stephens, responded to the writ with this statement:

> Texas Gulf Sulphur entered into a mining exploration agreement with Leitch . . . , providing for further investigation by Leitch of certain areas in the provinces of Ontario and Quebec over which Texas Gulf had previously conducted geophysical surveys. The areas concerned were clearly delineated on a plan attached to the agreement. Texas Gulf's recent base metal discovery in the township of Kidd . . . is not situated in any of the areas subject to the terms of such agreement. . . .

In the four and a half years before the case was decided, Leitch and Highland Bell Mines were the yo-yos of the Toronto Stock Exchange. Leitch once reached $15 during the trial; Highland Bell was as high as $18.50. The action of these stocks revealed a peculiar psychology among stock market speculators: The higher the price of Leitch and Highland Bell went, the more intense became the belief that the two companies really had a claim to the Kidd Creek Mine and this in turn produced even stranger touting of the stock by a number of usually conservative investment firms.

As an indication of just how far this went, even Newconex Holdings, the Canadian subsidiary of giant Consolidated Goldfields of South Africa, purchased a sizeable block of Leitch and Highland Bell stock. Newconex has never made any public comment on this unusual (for them) gamble, but a study of their annual statements suggests that they were sharp enough to sell out their holdings before the final collapse.

The exploration agreement, a not uncommon type in the mining business, called for Texas Gulf to turn over to Leitch information gathered from preliminary exploration of certain areas in Ontario and Quebec. Mostly, this was land that Texas Gulf had "flown" – the data took the form of electromagnetic readings taken during aerial surveys. In some locations, Texas Gulf had also done some exploration on the ground. Leitch was, in a sense, to "follow up" this work with a more intensive examination of its own. The exploration agreement was simply an exchange of information: No land ownership was involved. If Leitch found what it thought to be a mine, only then would it go about attempting to acquire rights to the property from whoever the owner might be. In the event Leitch did find a mine, and was able to get rights to the land, it would compensate Texas Gulf with a 10% interest in a new company which would be formed by Leitch to develop and operate the mine.

There was one other important element in the agreement: Once having turned over to Leitch its preliminary exploration data, Texas Gulf was for two years to stay off the surveyed areas except with the express written consent of Leitch.

Two and a half weeks after Texas Gulf announced the discovery of what was to be regarded as one of the world's largest base metals mines, Leitch wrote a letter enquiring whether Texas Gulf had acquired any right to lands in the surveyed areas covered by the exploration agreement and therefore out-of-bounds to Texas Gulf. The implicit question was: Had Texas Gulf found its mine on land to which it had ceded prior rights to Leitch?

Texas Gulf took 11 days to reply to this letter. On May 19, 1964, Texas Gulf told Leitch that no, it had not acquired any lands covered by the exploration agreement.

Leitch's statement of claim, filed in the Supreme Court of Ontario on September 1, 1964, said that the Kidd Creek mine lay in one of the 14 designated areas covered by the exploration agreement and therefore belonged to Leitch. There was no doubt, said Leitch, that the Kidd orebody lay within the confines of the area described by the agreement as "surveyed area 3 Prosser-Geary," and this was confirmed by the fact that Texas Gulf had turned over to Leitch airborne geophysical data covering the land where the mine was eventually found. Furthermore, said Leitch, Texas Gulf had gone on to acquire other properties surrounding the discovery site which also lay within the forbidden "surveyed area 3 Prosser-Geary."

In reply Texas Gulf told the court that "the exploration work which the defendant Texas Gulf has carried out is not within area 3 or any area with respect to which Leitch was given any rights under the said agreement. "It was true the Kidd Creek mine was discovered near the boundary of "surveyed area 3 Prosser-Geary," but in fact the mine lay within an adjoining "surveyed area 4 Timmins."

This was the essence of a dispute which took more than two years to adjudicate in what was to become the longest and biggest civil lawsuit in Canada's history. (But perhaps not the most principled. Just before the trial was to start, the president of Leitch discovered that someone had placed two electronic eavesdropping devices in the walls of his office. Later he discovered that his home phone was tapped.) In green-broad-loomed courtroom 20 on the top floor of the new court building on Toronto's University Avenue, the country's highest priced lawyers generated more than two million words of testimony and introduced more than 1,100 exhibits in a trial which lasted 130 days. Mr. Justice George A. Gale was subjected not only to days of heavy technical evidence from geologists and geophysicists, but also to the testimony of international map-reading experts and geographers who were called by both sides to argue where the Kidd Creek mine lay in relation to the several miles of common boundary between "surveyed area 3 Prosser-Geary" and "surveyed area 4 Timmins."

It was the most trying case Mr. Justice Gale had ever been called upon to decide. The emotions raised by the trial reached such a pitch, and the amount of money which went into speculation in Leitch stock was of such an amount, that when Gale announced his judgment eight months after the trial ended, he required a constant police guard for several months afterwards.

Texas Gulf had made the following "representations" in the prelude to its exploration agreement with Leitch:

(A) Texas Gulf conducted or caused to be conducted geophysical surveys of those portions of the Province of Quebec and the Province of Ontario, shown outlined in red on the plan attached hereto and marked 1, 3, 5, 6, 8, 9, 10, 11, 12, 13, 14, 15, 18, 19 respectively (hereinafter referred to collectively as the "surveyed areas"), and

(B) Texas Gulf has indicated on the said plan any and all geophysical anomalies on the surveyed areas detected by said aerial geophysical surveys, and

(C) Texas Gulf carried out ground geophysical and

geological surveys and diamond drilling on portions of the surveyed areas, and

(D) Texas Gulf prepared survey plans of the said aerial geophysical surveys and has prepared reports and plans of the said ground and geophysical and geological surveys and of said diamond drilling and has the right to enter into this agreement in respect to said survey plans, reports and plans.

These representations, as later became evident, were not accurate. In fact, representations (A) and (B) were almost entirely inaccurate.

The "attached plan," which was in fact a map, did not outline the surveyed areas in red. Nor did it indicate any anomalies which had been detected by Texas Gulf's aerial geophysical surveys. For these reasons, argued Leitch, the map – which had been prepared by Texas Gulf – "is a location or index plan only."

If that were the case, then the areas covered by the agreement would be decided by the data turned over by Texas Gulf to Leitch. And that data included aerial geophysical information gathered by flying over what was to become the Kidd Creek mine.

The 19 survey areas in Ontario and Quebec which had been "flown" by Texas Gulf were chosen on the basis of geological information gathered by geologist Leo Miller when Texas Gulf first began its Canadian Shield examination in 1957 and 1958. Each area was plotted on a map, and then the entire area was photographed from the air. The final photograph was really a mosaic, produced by piecing together a series of individual aerial photographs.

Onto this mosaic photograph would be drawn the boundaries of the area, and within those boundaries, a series of parallel lines along which the surveying aircraft was to travel.

The aircraft – in Texas Gulf's case, a helicopter – would fly along a straight line, turn around at the boundary of the area, and would fly back in a parallel course to the first flight line. Generally, these flight lines were spaced at one-quarter-mile intervals, a margin which was small enough to minimize the possibility that anomalies would lie between the flight lines and therefore go undetected.

Aboard the helicopter were three instruments: a motion picture camera, a machine which recorded variations in the conductivity of the earth, and an intervalometer to correlate the electromagnetic variations with the ground being photographed by the motion picture camera. From the information gathered by these instruments, Texas Gulf was able to transfer onto the photographic mosaic a reasonably accurate location of the anomalies found.

Later, airborne electromagnetic maps would be prepared to reflect the major topographic features, the flight paths of the aircraft, and variations in the lines traced by the electromagnetic recorder. The effect of this was a white piece of paper striped with parallel black lines which squiggled when an anomaly was encountered. All of this information, as it pertained to the surveyed areas covered in the exploration agreement, was turned over to Leitch by Texas Gulf.

"Surveyed area 4 Timmins" was one of the areas given priority by geologist Leo Miller following his geological examination of the Canadian shield in 1957 and 1958. In a report accompanying his recommendations, Miller mentioned a sulphide – and therefore potentially ore-bearing – zone in the northeastern part of Kidd Township. It was this early investigation by Miller which led to the decision to "fly" the land that later became known as "Surveyed area 4 Timmins." But when Miller laid out the boundaries of the area, he drew the northern boundary very, very close (1½ miles) to the sulphide zone.

The first flight over the Kidd 55 orebody was made on March 3, 1959. The helicopter flew over three known sulphide deposits in the area to test the equipment and calibrate the electromagnetic recorder. Then the helicopter flew over and recorded the anomaly which later proved to be the indication of the Kidd Creek mine. What happened, however, was that in some instances the flight paths of the helicopter did not quite reach the boundary between "surveyed area 4 Timmins" and "surveyed area 3 Prosser-Geary." This was a not uncommon error which, five years later, was to lead to the Leitch litigation.

In 1960 Miller suggested in a report to his superiors that the entire region of favorable geology north of Timmins had not been covered by airborne survey the previous year. He recommended that an adjoining area – which was to become known as "surveyed area 3 Prosser-Geary" be traversed by helicopter survey. It was also Miller's suggestion that, while this new flight survey was being made, it would be well to extend it over to Timmins area 4 to pick up those locations that had been missed in the 1959 flights.

As a result the photographic mosaic prepared for the 1960 flight survey had a piece added for the specific purpose of reflying the Kidd 55 anomaly. On June 21, 1960, Texas Gulf's helicopter again flew over the Kidd 55 zone, and the information gathered was included on the electromagnetic tapes and the motion picture film. These tapes and film, according to custom, were placed in a labelled brown paper envelope for future reference.

Three years later, this envelope with many others was stored on a high shelf in Texas Gulf's Canadian exploration headquarters in Calgary, Alberta. Three days after the execution of the exploration agreement, Leitch's chief geologist, tall, handsome Charles Pegg, traveled to Calgary to pick up the aerial exploration data which was to be turned over to his company. Texas Gulf claim that by error, John Macdougall, a Texas Gulf employee, gave Pegg the envelope which included the data from the June 21, 1960, reflight over the Kidd zone.

Charles Pegg described the incident to me quite differently:

That afternoon I went into the main Texas Gulf office suite with Macdougall and met all the various Texas Gulf personnel there. Podolsky, Macdougall and I went into a small interior office and there Podolsky climbed up a ladder and brought down boxes containing these brown envelopes. He sorted them himself. If it was one we were supposed to have, he put it on one side, and if it was one we weren't to have, he put it on the other side. Podolsky was familiar with all the material and he did the sorting very slowly and deliberately. When he gave me the Kidd material, it could hardly have been an accident.

By the time the trial began on October 31, 1966, everyone agreed that the Kidd orebody did not lie in surveyed area 3 Prosser-Geary. There was no doubt that the mine lay within surveyed area 4 Timmins, as drawn on the map attached to the exploration agreement.

However, Leitch argued that this map, because it did not have the surveyed areas outlined in red and because it did not show the presence of anomalies, as Texas Gulf had represented in the agreement, was not meant to be definitive in terms of the areas covered by the exploration agreement. Leitch further submitted that it was entitled to any and all lands flown by the Prosser-Geary survey of 1960 – and that included the property where the Kidd Creek mine was situated. Leitch attempted to exploit what it said was an ambiguity in the words "surveyed area 3 Prosser-Geary": Did that mean area 3 as laid out on the map, or the Prosser Geary survey as it was actually flown?

It was Texas Gulf's position that the map attached to the

exploration agreement was the effective and controlling instrument. They said there was no ambiguity in the words "surveyed area 3 Prosser-Geary," but even if there were, the reflight over the Kidd 55 zone in 1960, though it did take place at the same time as the Prosser Geary survey, was not really part of that survey.

Before the trial began, several brokerage firms hired lawyers to examine the pleadings of both parties. Attempts were also made to follow proceedings before the court, although most of the observers soon gave up because of the welter of technical evidence. In any case it was not possible to arrive independently at a consensus on the basis of the evidence. What was required, as Mr. Justice Gale said afterwards, was a judicial interpretation of the exploration agreement. That meant that, first of all, a judge had to try to ascertain the meaning and effect of the exploration agreement, and the scope of its intended application. If that was not clear, then the court would have to decide the meaning of the contract in the light of what the intentions of Texas Gulf and Leitch had been.

Ultimately, it boiled down that the judge had to choose between the contradictory testimony of two men.

The high risk entailed in attempting to forecast the outcome of the trial didn't deter all brokerage firms. Several counseled their clients that the orebody hanging in the balance was so valuable that it was important to be sure of a share in the profits; therefore, they reasoned, it was the course of wisdom to buy shares of both Texas Gulf and Leitch.

Lafferty, Harwood and Company, an investment firm based in Montreal, pursued a much more ambitious and dangerous course. A senior partner in the firm, Richard Lafferty, decided that the stakes were so high that he would make a special attempt to follow the proceedings and make his own value judgments. As a result of this, Lafferty sent out a series of 51 letters commenting on the case, letters that went to 365 clients including the personnel of 140 institutional investors in Canada, the United States and Europe. The first letter was dated November 24, 1965, almost a year before the arguments were to begin in open court. It said:

> If Leitch were to win its full claim of $450 million, it would increase the breakup value of the shares by $83.70, compared to the current [market] price of $6.15. . . .
>
> Outside of this formal presentation [the pleadings] by both the plaintiff and the defendant, there is additional circumstantial evidence that has had some influence on our thinking. First there is the general character of the principals of Leitch, who have been in the mining industry for many years. They are well respected in the industry. They have a lot of experience and we have seen no historical evidence of frivolous obstructionism by them in the past. . . .
>
> In contrast, the management of Texas Gulf were not, up to this time, active in prospecting for mines in Ontario. . . .

When the trial began, Lafferty made frequent trips from Montreal to Toronto, a distance of 350 miles, to witness the proceedings. Frequently his letters recounted portions of the transcript. Often Lafferty interjected his own comments about such things as the credibility of witnesses. From the beginning, he was confident that Leitch would win its claim. In letter No. 8, less than five months after the trial began, he reported to his subscribers:

> If we were to make a judgment at this stage as to what the outcome of the trial is likely to be, based on the entire claim made by Leitch, our view expressed as a

percentage judgment after having read the transcript evidence of the trial to date would be 85 per cent in favor of Leitch and 15 per cent in favor of Texas Gulf.

Lafferty lengthened his odds even more with this comment:

We allow the 15 per cent to Texas Gulf not on what has been presented so far, but what might be unexpectedly presented. Again, we should caution that this is the view of a financial analyst and not a trial lawyer.

Lafferty, Harwood's reputation as a shrewd brokerage firm was acknowledged in the investment community. Undoubtedly, large purchases of Leitch stock were made as a result of his inaccurate view of Leitch's chances. Karl Springer had a more cautious outlook. Between April, 1967, and November, 1968, he sold thousands of shares of Leitch stock at the then inflated prices.

The first business contact between Texas Gulf and Leitch had been in 1961 in Princeton, British Columbia, when a Texas Gulf geologist, David Lowrie, encountered Charles Pegg, the exploration manager for Leitch. The two men discussed how their companies might somehow co-ordinate their exploration efforts. Almost one year later, Lowrie and Pegg met once again in the Engineers' Club in Toronto. Lowrie told Pegg Texas Gulf would be willing to turn over some of its preliminary exploration data in return for a 10% share of the profits if Leitch found a mine. The hard bargaining to follow was conducted between Pegg and Walter Holyk, Texas Gulf's senior geologist.

When Pegg wrote to Holyk with reference to a possible exploration agreement in February, 1963, Holyk replied that Texas Gulf had performed "a number of scattered surveys" and "would be willing to discuss turning over data in any area with a possible temporary restriction on some ground north of Timmins." Holyk's reply enclosed a map, showing areas that had been surveyed by Texas Gulf. In mid-March the two men met at Toronto's Royal York Hotel at a convention of the Prospectors and Developers Association, and discussed the terms of a proposed contract. With the map spread before them on a coffee table, they discussed the various survey areas, what prospects they held, and how much work Texas Gulf had done on them. This meeting was crucial to the testimony at the later trial; there is no question that the dispute turned on the nature of the discussions in that hotel room. In some respects, particularly in regard to the talk concerning "surveyed area 4 Timmins," the testimony of Pegg and Holyk was flatly contradictory.

In the week or so following the Royal York meeting, Pegg prepared a number of draft agreements, sending one to Holyk. He suggested in a covering letter that Texas Gulf should prepare a map to be attached to the agreement. Holyk gave instructions for a map to be prepared; when it was finished, he noticed that the surveyed areas were not outlined in red as described in the agreement, but were filled in with different colors to indicate the years each area had been surveyed. Holyk thought this was a better method anyway, and so let it go to Pegg unchanged.

Following a continuing exchange of the draft agreement between Pegg and Holyk, during which some minor alterations were made, a final draft was submitted for approval to Texas Gulf's Exploration Manager, R. D. Mollison. Mollison approved the changes, and passed the agreement on to Senior Vice-president, Charles Fogarty. Fogarty later said that he assured himself that the agreement would not include any part of surveyed area 4 Timmins, and affixed the initials "C.F.F." Meantime, copies of the final draft were also under consideration by lawyers for both Texas Gulf and Leitch.

Unknown to either Pegg or Holyk, who were preoccupied

with the minor alterations in the body of the agreement, some-body had drastically altered the representations which formed the preamble to the agreement. For that reason, Texas Gulf's representations in reference to the attached map were not accurate. It is probable that these changes were made by one of Leitch's lawyers.

The trial ended on April 25, 1968, with Leitch shares trading at $9.50 and Texas Gulf stock at $134.

On the same day, in Houston, Texas, the directors of Texas Gulf Sulphur Company tripled the quarterly dividend rate to 30¢ per share. A statement by President Claude Stephens included only one sentence about operations at the Kidd Creek mine – which were going ahead in blissful disregard of the Leitch lawsuit. Stephens discussed at some length, however, the rise in the price of sulphur, which was by now $42 a long ton.

It had taken Mr. Justice George Gale seven months to prepare his 167-page judgment in the Texas Gulf-Leitch case. During that period a special force was assigned from the Ontario Provincial Police and the Metropolitan Toronto Police to maintain a 24-hour security check. The judge's courthouse suite was guarded around the clock. Special blinds were hung on the windows of the suite so that even window-washers could not see inside. Electronic equipment was in-stalled to jam any "bugs" that may have been planted in or around the offices. There were stringent security checks on all persons involved in the preparation and printing of the judgment.

Despite all these precautions there apparently was a leak. On Wednesday, November 27, 1968, Texas Gulf stock suddenly began to trade in large volume on the New York Stock Exchange, and this continued through Friday, November 29, 1968. On that day, at seven o'clock in the evening, after the west coast stock markets had closed, the word went out that Mr. Justice Gale would release his judgment later that evening.

A crowd of lawyers and reporters gathered to hear the judge. He began, "I think we all know why we're here," and he then read the conclusion of his judgment:

There will be judgment dismissing the plaintiff's claim for a declaration that the defendant holds the Kidd Creek Mine as constructive trustee for Leitch and also dismissing the alternative claim for damages for breach of contract with respect to the mine itself.

Gale had decided there was no ambiguity in the exploration agreement, and that in any case it had always been the intention of the involved parties that the surveyed area 4 Timmins was to be specifically excluded from the agreement. In this regard he chose to reject the evidence of Leitch's Charles Pegg wherever it differed materially from the testimony of Walter Holyk*. This decision of credibility was a major factor in deciding that the $2 billion orebody belonged to the huge U.S. firm rather than to Karl Springer's tiny Canadian company. Gale's decision was not happily received at the Toronto Stock Exchange.

Before Gale went to sleep that night there were four tele-

---

*Excerpts from the Gale judgment. 1. About Charles Pegg: "Mr. Pegg's recollection of the large storage room where he spent almost 3 and a half days was quite faulty. He described it as a room 20 feet wide and 30 feet long whereas it is 25 feet wide and 58 feet long. While the misdescription was not monumental, it is strange that it would be given by a person who boasted that he had a good recollection of all that occurred in Calgary...." (p. 52.) "Then too Mr. Pegg was rather equivocal about it. On his examination for discovery he said that he could not 'recall' the incident, whereas at the trial he denied it most emphatically – almost eagerly. . . ." (p. 46.) 2. About Walter Holyk: "Some of his testimony at the trial was not entirely consistent with that given by him in the proceedings brought by the Securities and Exchange Commission in the United States, but those inconsistencies were not of such a nature as to induce me to think that Dr. Holyk was falsifying his evidence in this case." (p. 54.) "There is one other trifling point that might be mentioned. While Dr. Holyk said that he had outlined the areas in Exhibit 9B in red, in fact it was Mr. Pegg who did that. I regard that as an insignificant mistake on the part of the former." (p. 55.)

phone threats on his life. During the following months, wherever he went – to court, to cocktail parties, on shopping trips with his wife – he was accompanied by plainclothes police officers.

On the Monday following Gale's dismissal of the Leitch claim, Texas Gulf Sulphur was by far the most active stock on the New York Stock Exchange, rising $3 to $39.12. (The stock had been split three-for-one in the intervening period; the price was the equivalent of $117.37 on the old shares.) In Toronto, trading in shares of Leitch was delayed for two and a half hours; Leitch began trading at $3.50, down $8.75 from the preceding stock market day. Thus the Gale judgment slashed more than $25 million from the market's valuation of the three million Leitch shares. A like amount was cut from the market value of Leitch's subsidiary and co-plaintiff, Highland Bell Mines Ltd.

All that was left was the small chance afforded by an appeal, and the directors of Leitch quickly dismissed this, despite the fact that the cost of an appeal would have been only a small fraction of the estimated $600,000 legal bill already pending as a result of the first trial. Shareholders were told:

> With the utmost respect to the Chief Justice, your directors do not agree with much of the reasoning and many of the observations contained in the judgment of the Chief Justice and your directors retain full confidence in Mr. Charles Pegg.
>
> However, we are advised by our lawyers that, because of the limitations on the powers of an appellate court to interfere with findings of fact made by a trial judge, the further heavy expense involved in an appeal would not be justified.

So died Karl Springer's dream and with it the hopes of thousands of Canadian stockholders.

Chapter Eighteen

THE SCENE WIDENS

Stock in Texas Gulf Sulphur Company had not been exactly a wallflower on the New York Stock Exchange in the more than four decades since it had been granted listing privileges. On the other hand, it was hardly what modern jargon would call a go-go stock. Among the 64,918 shareholders at the end of 1963 (a reduction of almost 7,000 from the year before) were a goodly number of widows and orphans. The fortunes of the company had been predictable, insofar as the market for sulphur could be forecast, and it was not uncommon for investment counselors to comment (as one did in February, 1964, still completely ignorant of the Timmins discovery) that there was a direct relationship between the price of TGS stock and the supply-demand balance in the world sulphur market.

The stock had come up from its low of $11.50 in late 1962, and during 1963 had risen more or less steadily to about $25. Over the past 10 years, the average price-to-earnings ratio of Texas Gulf shares had been less than 14; the fact that it had risen to a less conservative level of about 25 times earnings was giving some analysts cause to hesitate to recommend it.

A more daring approach was taken by F. S. Smithers and Company, which in February, 1964, recommended the stock in spite of the fact it had almost doubled during 1963:

> To recommend the shares of Texas Gulf Sulphur now that they are $23 [the 1963 low had been $13.75], and in view of the somewhat checkered history of the company, requires considerable faith in two fundamentals. The first of these is that the outlook for the sulphur industry has improved; and the second is that there is a reasonable chance that the 'non-sulphur' enterprises undertaken over the past several years will be successful.

After considering the prospect of firmer prices for sulphur, Smithers went on:

> The 'non-sulphur' enterprises to which we allude are, in particular, the Moab [Utah] potash properties and the phosphate mining and processing experiments now being undertaken in the Carolinas. (We recognize the company is active in oil exploration and development, and in the search for other materials, but at the moment, these are not fundamental to our concept and therefore are given very short shrift in this memorandum.)

This en passant approach to Texas Gulf's non-sulphur ventures well expressed the investment community's attitude, hardened by the company's historic reliance on sulphur, that the fortunes of Texas Gulf were inextricably linked with the sulphur market.

It helps to explain why, when Texas Gulf shares were barely embarked on their rise to an ultimate price of more than $140 each, the *New York Times* quoted the caution of one New York broker:

> A Wall Street observer said yesterday that TGS might have a real bonanza in its strike in Ontario, "but every $10 advance in the price of the stock is equivalent to $100 million since the company has 10 million shares outstanding. That's a lot of money on a mining claim, which is a depleting asset."

In spite of this fretful atmosphere, the April 16 discovery announcement made Texas Gulf the 1964 sensation of the stock market. In 1963, 3,553,300 shares of the company changed hands on the New York Stock Exchange; in 1964 Texas Gulf traded 24,221,700 shares and was by far the most active issue on the Big Board, far outbusying the shares of such immensely bigger corporations as Chrysler, Radio Corporation of America, and American Telephone and Telegraph. On one day, April 30, 906,700 TGS shares were traded. There had been nothing to compare with that since 941,000 shares of Allegheny Corp, traded in the midst of a proxy fight two years before.

Texas Gulf's Secretary, David Crawford, had bought 600 shares for himself and his wife when the market opened on the morning of April 16. He later told a court that he had no misgivings about the purchase of the stock; he was aware of the story that had been published that morning in the *Northern Miner*, and he had been given to understand that the Minister of Mines for Ontario had announced the discovery on television in Canada the night before. Being a lawyer, Crawford knew the provision of Section 16 of the Securities Exchange Act, that he would have to report his purchases publicly, and that any stock market profits he might make within six months would be subject to forfeiture. Still, he thought it appropriate to inform Harold Kline, general counsel for Texas Gulf, of his purchase. Crawford finally made contact in the evening at Kline's New York apartment.

That day, while the press conference was in progress at Texas Gulf's midtown office in the Pan-Am Building, the New York Stock Exchange delayed trading in the company's shares. When trading was permitted to resume, the price of the stock jumped $7.62 to $37. (The purchases described earlier had been made on the Midwest Stock Exchange.) By the end of the day, Texas Gulf shares were $36.37, highest closing price since 1957. The trading volume was 442,000, more than three times the next most active issue, RCA. In Toronto, the *Telegram*'s headline was "METAL FIND TRIGGERS STOCK BOOM," and a final edition bulletin carried the news that Toronto Stock Exchange trading volume had set a record 16,659,000 shares – most of it related to companies with land near Texas Gulf's Kidd Township property.

At the New York Stock Exchange, officials took note of the activity in Texas Gulf shares and invited Executive Vice-president Charles Fogarty to discussions the following day. Company Counsel Harold Kline, went along, as did secretary David Crawford. Representing the New York Stock Exchange were Phillip West and Merle Wick, Vice-presidents, Lee Arning, Assistant Director of the Department of Member Brokerage Firms, and Anthony Burger, of the Department of Stock List.

There was some mild apprehension at the meeting about a possible intervention by the Securities and Exchange Commission. But it was not a feeling of guilt; it was simply the forbidding prospect that the company would now get into long discussions and explanations for the benefit of the SEC. The matter of Texas Gulf's drilling on the Kidd property was not at issue. What the stock exchange officials were most interested in was the set of circumstances which prompted first the April 12 cautionary press release, and four days later, the announcement of a major discovery.

In the course of his explanation Charles Fogarty did say, "Up to this time [April 11] I can say that there wasn't even a member of our board that knew we were even on the scent of something, because we just go about our business in as methodical a manner as possible. . . ."

The minutes of this meeting on Friday, April 17, were stenographically recorded, and they include this statement attributed to the NYSE's Arning:

> . . . If you can say none of our insiders bought or sold a share of stock, I think it would be helpful. We certainly should know, and I am sure the SEC is going to ask. Mr. Jaegerman [Edward Jaegerman, top Investigative Attorney for the SEC] is going to see you today, and he will want to find out exactly what was this. I think all of your key people, officers and directors, all ought to be covered.

Texas Gulf of course was not able to give any such assurance, but Charles Fogarty replied, "I will try and let Mr. Burger know."

As Fogarty later recalled the circumstances, he said that on entering the meeting, one of the stock exchange representatives asked, "Would you tell us a little bit about TGS?" and "I talked as fast as I could for about 30 minutes and tried to give him as much information about TGS and the events of the 12th and the 16th releases as it was possible to in that short period of time, at which time we were interrupted by someone stating there is a crisis in Curtis Publishing Company on the [trading] floor. . . ."

Curtis Publishing had lost $18.9 million in 1962, chiefly because its flagship publication, the *Saturday Evening Post*, had been losing advertisers and readers. The company cut its loss to $3.4 million in 1963, and now the chairman and president, Matthew Culligan, was forecasting a profit for the first three months of 1964. The stock market wasn't much impressed with this turnaround. Shares of Curtis in the spring of 1964 were only a dollar or two higher than the trough of $5.50 reached the year before. Investors were understandably sceptical about the optimistic face that Curtis turned towards the outside world; they were afraid that the enthusiasm was artificial and that it was for the benefit of advertisers and subscribers.

What interrupted the April 17 meeting between Texas Gulf officers and officials of the New York Stock Exchange was the vigorous stock market response to a statement by Curtis's Culligan. He revealed, for the first time, an agreement with Texas Gulf for mineral exploration of a portion of Curtis's timberlands in the Timmins area. The Culligan announcement was at first sketchy, but it soon became known that part of the Curtis lands were within a few hundred feet of the "eye" of the Texas Gulf discovery. That was all Wall Street needed. On April 17, while Texas Gulf was climbing a further $3.87 to $40.25, Curtis stock was creating its own sensation, jumping $2.62 to $11. Within two weeks, Curtis reached $17.50.

Throughout this rise, Curtis officials – still, no doubt, with advertisers in mind as much as shareholders – protested that the company was returning to soundness aside from any benefits from the Timmins properties. Matthew Culligan said "a great amount of good news about Curtis" was buried amid the furor over the ore discovery, and he added:

Our circulation is either stable or increasing, the cover prices of all our magazines [*Post, Ladies Home Journal, Holiday, American Home*, and *Jack and Jill*] are stable or being raised, first quarter advertising was up in all magazines, and our Sharon Hill [Pennsylvania] printing plant is the most efficient in the nation.

A much different perspective was put on the Curtis-Texas Gulf deal in later months when some Curtis shareholders attacked the exploration agreement and issued complaints against Curtis management on the basis that the company should have got more for its property. In its defence, Curtis then invoked a statement by its new president, John M. Clifford, who detailed the salutary effects of a $24 million purchase by Texas Gulf of Curtis timberlands:

> Well, the first reason is that the board of directors felt that we were getting a fair price, that we were getting a good deal out of the properties that we were selling, bearing in mind that Curtis Publishing Company is in the publishing business.
>
> . . . We have protected our source of supply as far as pulp wood is concerned at no additional cost to Curtis, and the $24 million which we expect to receive for these particular assets will enable us to reduce our bank loans, which together with one other deal this year will leave Curtis owing between $4 million and $4½ million.
>
> Since the announcement [of the agreement with Texas Gulf] Curtis' business has improved substantially in all of our magazines. It is up between 30 and 40 per cent on the *Post*, for example. . . . We have on our books, as of a week or 10 days ago as a result of this, a better atmosphere, between $5 million and $6 million extra business that has come.
>
> We are dealing in a business in which – whether it is right or wrong – it is a fact that in the advertising business, a great deal depends on the psychology of what is going on. . . . We, through what we have done with our finances this year . . . have suddenly, in the eyes of

the people on Madison Avenue, become acceptable again, and it results in doing better business.

In other words, this particular deal will enable Curtis to turn the corner, and become a profitable enterprise. That is the background that has influenced us and our board in working so hard to make this deal.

Curtis had acquired its interests in the timberlands surrounding Timmins in 1945, through a wholly-owned subsidiary, T. S. Woollings and Company. Curtis was well aware of the mineral potential of the area, and long before Texas Gulf came along had negotiated for the sale of mineral rights to these lands. In fact, in 1953 and 1954 Curtis, with other companies, had formed the Prosser Syndicate and had conducted geophysical surveys on Woollings properties. The result of these surveys was to do no further exploration, but to try, if possible, to interest large mining companies to carry out further tests. Talks with McIntyre Porcupine Mines, one of the world's biggest gold producers, fell through in 1956 or 1957. Similarly, nothing came of negotiations with the International Nickel Company of Canada. In both cases, Woollings was anxious that it be paid an acreage rental; Curtis needed the money, and it would be an incentive for the lessee to get to work.

Curtis Publishing had suffered the first loss in its 70-year history in 1961. Super-salesman Culligan joined the company in July, 1962, as president and chairman, to win back the loyalty of advertisers. He personally arranged to call on the nation's 120 largest advertisers, he cut spending and dropped personnel in an organization that was ridden with dead wood and creaking with inefficiency, and he reorganized Curtis management into four management teams: books, magazines, circulation, and printing and production.

Culligan remembered thinking it "strange" when he was

first approached by a "large company" interested in Curtis' timberlands. Nothing came of this encounter, nor was there any fruit from discussions with Texas Gulf in 1962. In November, 1963, Texas Gulf geologist Ken Darke walked into the office of Woollings President, Arthur L. Bennett, and that meeting led to an agreement five months later covering the land southeast of the Murray Hendrie estate. Culligan had no idea that beneath that lot lay 6,500,000 tons of copper-zinc-silver ore worth almost $20 million.

That early agreement gave Texas Gulf exclusive rights to explore 46,354 acres of Curtis lands, and provided that Texas Gulf relinquish one-third of the land each year and pay rent for the first year of 25¢ per acre. Texas Gulf also got as part of the deal an option to purchase the mineral rights to any 1,920 acres of the land for $50,000 in Canadian funds and 10% of any profits from mining operations on Curtis lands.

Woollings, the Curtis subsidiary which negotiated the agreement, had not even been aware that Texas Gulf had been drilling and otherwise exploring neighboring property in Kidd Township.

On the day Texas Gulf announced its discovery, April 16, 1964, the company was courteous enough to telephone Woollings president, Arthur Bennett, to inform him that he had sold land within 300 feet of the drill hole that had struck one of the world's richest base metals mines. Curtis sought advice from Canadian mining experts and lawyers, but found to its dismay that the deal with Texas Gulf was binding, and that furthermore, Texas Gulf had no duty to disclose to Curtis its next-door discovery.

The stock market fury in shares of Curtis in the summer of 1964 was the last moment of glory for Matthew Culligan. Surrounded by a tradition-bound executive superstructure (which included 25 vice-presidents) and jarred by an editorial revolt, Culligan was ousted as president and chief executive officer. It was left to his successor, former television network vice-president, John M. Clifford, to oversee the subsequent outright sale of most of Curtis's timber and mineral holdings.

It was this deal that was later attacked as injudicious by some Curtis shareholders, but it had its attractive aspects for the publishing firm that was mired in bank debts. Curtis certainly needed the money, and Texas Gulf was anxious to buy Curtis's 10% share of the mining profits.

During 1965 Curtis retained independent appraisers who reported that the 10% share of that part of the Kidd Creek mine beneath the former Woollings property was worth between $6 million and $7 million. The appraisers put a value of $2,500,000 on Curtis's other timber holdings in Canada, and a value of $7,800,000 on Pennsylvania woodlands owned through another subsidiary. When Texas Gulf paid $24 million it was about $7 million in excess of the total appraised value. That revenue was almost enough to offset Curtis's $28 million bank debt – and it might have saved the *Saturday Evening Post*; it certainly postponed its demise.

Coming when it did and producing both a huge sum of money plus a resurgence of confidence, the Texas Gulf discovery may very well have saved the Curtis empire from a complete collapse.

There were other, less direct beneficiaries of the Texas Gulf strike. A week after announcement of the discovery, shares of International Nickel jumped $5.50 because, according to the *New York Times*, "it was confirmed the company had an interest in an ore discovery near Timmins." Even in the excitement of the moment this was stretching a point – what Inco had done was acquire mineral rights to 140,000 acres starting about 1½ miles north of Kidd Township.

Pennzoil Company, now known as Pennzoil United Inc. because of a recent merger with United Gas Inc., is an integrated (wellhead-to-consumer) oil company with production assets throughout the United States and in Alberta, where it owns most of Triad Oil. In addition, Pennzoil, under that brand name, is a nationwide distributor of motor oils and lubricants. It has had about 10,000 shareholders for the past few years.

Within a year of the Texas Gulf announcement, Pennzoil Company had made a pre-tax profit of $4,297,769 on the purchase and sale of 145,700 TGS shares, which gives a profit equivalent to about $340 per Pennzoil shareholder.

Clinton Williams Murchison Jr. (pronounced Murkison), and his brother, John Dabney Murchison, are in their mid-forties, the sons of Texas wheeler-dealer oilman Clint Murchison Sr. They are probably best known outside of Texas for winning control of Allegheny Corp. from Woolworth heir Allan P. Kirby in 1961, in one of the most hard-fought and widely publicized proxy battles of all time. Allegheny then had control of, among other things, New York Central Railroad, and Minneapolis' Investors Diversified Services, a $3.4 billion investment octopus whose interests include the world's biggest mutual funds. Their father, now about 73, got rich buying oil leases in partnership with the famous Sid Richardson. The younger Murchisons are among the U.S.'s biggest residential builders; they own insurance firms, banks, hotels, country clubs, a publishing firm, and oil and gas companies.

The two brothers, Clint and John, bought 100,000 shares of Texas Gulf stock before the April 16 announcement at prices between $20 and $22 per share; their holdings a year later had risen in value from $2 million to over $7 million.

In the days following the discovery announcement, Texas Gulf shares moved higher by instinct. It was one thing to know that the company had found an "indicated" 25 million tons of copper-zinc-silver, and to be able to calculate the gross value of that orebody. It was another to be able to translate the meaning of the orebody in terms of Texas Gulf's future earnings. Some directors of the company itself admitted later that they were not competent to evaluate the April 16 press release in this context, and there was no proof that many members of the investment community's research establishment were any better capable of doing so. There were too many imponderables beyond the grasp of even investment experts. Twenty-five million tons of $32 ore multiplied roughly to $850 million, a nice round figure which, however, did not take into account extraction, processing, shipping and marketing costs. Much also depended upon the company's plans for production— when, and at what rate.

There was also the confusion of the moment, and it led to frequent contradictions in the wide press coverage. The *New York Times* of April 17 quoted Exploration Vice-president Richard Mollison as "conservatively" estimating a $10 profit per ton of ore. Within days, President Claude Stephens disavowed that estimate and said, "We have never made any statement regarding profitability from the Canadian discovery."

Only one unanimous investment judgment was made concerning Texas Gulf: The Kidd Township find had made its shares a stock that could be blindly bought. Before the discovery announcement, the Value Line Investment Survey was of the opinion that "retention of Texas Gulf shares at their currently high price would not appear advisable." Value Line gave Texas Gulf its lowest rating for growth, for performance, and for potential. As the price of Texas Gulf shares rose, so did Value Line's appraisal. By the time the stock was up to $96 in May of 1966, Value Line was saying the price would be an average $158 in the three- to-five-year future.

In the third week of April, 1964, Texas Gulf was ill prepared for the saturation of publicity and the barrage of queries that transpired from announcement of the Kidd 55 discovery. It was notable that this $64 million corporation had no internal public relations staff. The toughest question Texas Gulf had been in the habit of fielding was the prospect for sulphur supply and demand, but this new situation was one that would have posed problems even for a publicity Svengali. Texas Gulf had customarily held its annual meetings in Houston, and generally they were dull, routine affairs, ill attended and accompanied by ritual rather than an exchange of information. On April 23, more than 300 persons attended the annual meeting at the Houston Club, and that number included as many newsmen as shareholders. There were persistent queries about a second discovery, and some newspapers stubbornly confused the high silver values at Kidd 55 with the supposed knowledge that Texas Gulf, subsequent to its acquisition of desirable land in the Timmins area, had found a silver mine as well. Sam Weiner, the business editor of the *Houston Post*, reflected the sense of letdown when he reported:

> An excited hubbub – but few nuggets – rewarded Texas Gulf Sulphur Company shareholders at their annual meeting. . . . One shareholder asked, "Is there any gold there?" and president Stephens replied, "No evidence of gold." "Much silver?" asked another anxious shareholder, and executive vice-president Fogarty responded with, "Some, but we can't say how much." And he added: "On the limited data we have, to try to say how much could be misleading."

Fogarty was already smarting from the criticism of some newspapers who had compared the April 12 and April 16 releases and who decided that Texas Gulf was being less than candid.

The meeting may have had an aspect of anticlimax, but it wasn't evident from the stock market performance of Texas Gulf shares. On April 23 the stock jumped $5.62 to a high of $48.25.

A week later, Texas Gulf came into its first official contact with the Securities and Exchange Commission. It was not a portentous affair, and was interpreted by the company as a routine, although slightly disconcerting, visit from SEC representatives. There was even the thought that the SEC was preoccupied with the possibility that Texas Gulf had been premature, rather than belated with its news about Kidd 55. Stephens instructed Fogarty in advance to furnish the commission with all available information. The meeting took place in the board room, across the hall from the offices of Stephens and Fogarty. The commission's Chief Mining Engineer, Benjamin Adelstein, brought along an assistant; the third SEC official was Edward Jaegerman. For Texas Gulf, Charles Fogarty did most of the talking. Counsel Harold Kline was at the meeting during the afternoon, and Claude Stephens spent about an hour there. Stephens spoke for a few minutes about the general prospects of the Timmins mine:

> I expressed our extreme confidence in the project. I outlined in a general way the work that we had put into this project. I outlined generally the amount of time that we had been exploring in the whole area for sulphide ores. I outlined in a very brief way, to the extent that I could, however, the manner in which we rather anticipated that this facility may come into production.

Then, according to Stephens, Adelstein said "he agreed with the April 12 release that at the time the release was filed for publication he would have had the same thing to say, that he couldn't have said any more at the time." Stephens remembered that Adelstein had said earlier that the release was "accurate" or "entirely correct." That was a statement that was to be hotly disputed by Adelstein and the Securities and Exchange Commission almost a year later, when the SEC shook the investment world with charges against Texas Gulf Sulphur Company and 13 of its employees.

Chapter Nineteen

THE SEC MOVES IN

It was not long before news of the inquiries by the Securities and Exchange Commission leaked out to the public. Inevitably the reports made headlines, but no one could have contemplated that the government agency, to use the words of one of its lawyers, was about to "explore new territory" in an attempt to impose new and more rigid responsibilities on corporate officers and directors – and even on lowly employees. Texas Gulf might have looked like another case of possible insider abuse, but the word "scandal" was never associated with the company until the SEC laid civil charges against Texas Gulf and 13 of its officers and employees four days before what was to have been a jubilant annual meeting in April, 1965.

In 1964 the company had accomplished the long-awaited reversal of the decline of profits. Its sales had risen to $70,369,732 from $62,248,521 in 1963; and net profit consequently had climbed to $11,556,189 or $1.15 per share from $9,353,652 or 93¢ per share. The price of sulphur, increased by $2 a ton on Jan. 1, 1965, was due for another boost. Texas Gulf had begun production at its North Carolina phosphate mine, and the first revenues were coming in from exploitation of the potash deposits at Moab, Utah. "In many respects," President Claude Stephens was to say, "1964 will go down in history as the beginning of a new era for the company." The annual report for 1964, while it was prepared in advance of the SEC charges, nevertheless suggested a corporate consciousness of public and government suspicions concerning the discovery of the Kidd Creek mine. It began:

> 1964 was an unusually eventful year for your company. Public interest naturally tended to focus on the spectacular success of our exploration team in Ontario, Canada. Important as this zinc-copper-silver-sulphide ore body is, however, it should not overshadow significant events of the year in other areas of our planned program of diversification and expansion.

One can only guess what care and forethought went into the preparation of that opening remark.

By the spring of 1965, the Ontario government had begun its own investigation into the sordid circumstances of the Windfall Oils and Mines affair. The Windfall inquiry had fateful consequences for Texas Gulf; the revelations it inspired may in fact have provided the motive for the SEC charges. Until the Windfall investigators began to delve into the affairs of geologist Ken Darke, it was not known to the public that the discovery hole on Kidd 55 had been drilled as early as November, 1963. It had not been thought to connect the first indication of the orebody with anything other than the press releases which emerged almost six months later. *Time* magazine had been under this general misapprehension shortly after the April 16, 1964, discovery announcement. In a masterpiece of inaccuracy, it reported:

> Just before Easter, Texas Gulf Sulphur Co. geologist Kenneth Dark stumbled out of the snow-packed bush near Timmins, Ont., jeeped twelve miles into town and placed a midnight call to the company's chief geologist in Stamford, Conn.

Apart from some incidental inaccuracies – Darke's name was misspelled, there was no snow on the ground, the telephone call was placed long before midnight – *Time* was of the understanding, like most other people, that the April press releases came hard on the heels of the discovery hole.

The Windfall inquiry deflated some of these myths: Texas Gulf chief geologist Walter Holyk was pressed to reveal the date of the discovery hole, and to interpret the meaning of the first core from Kidd-55-1. It wasn't long before the SEC's Edward Jaegerman was on the scene to follow more closely the proceedings at the Windfall royal commission.

On April 19, 1965, the Securities and Exchange Commission released its bombshell. Its first charge was that the release of April 12, 1964, was known to be "materially false and misleading." The second complaint concerned 13 individual defendants, and alleged that they had bought stock, caused others to buy stock, or were granted stock options during a period in which material facts concerning the company were concealed from the public. It was enough that a $220 million corporation had become the target of court charges laid by a government agency. What set the business community on its ear were other aspects of the complaint. For one thing, the SEC, acting on the mandate granted by the Securities Exchange

Act of 1934, was not only pursuing its traditional course of seeking injunctions against allegedly illegal practices, but was also taking upon itself the responsibility – previously left up to wronged shareholders – to attempt to eliminate what it considered to be ill-gotten gains. The SEC, in other words, asked the courts to force the defendants to give up their stock market profits. There was another ramification: The SEC wanted the insiders to also be responsible for the return of all stock market profits made by "tippees" – persons to whom the insiders allegedly transmitted private information of the discovery. (In a precedent of many years' standing, the SEC had held the tippees themselves responsible for their profits. In that case, a director of the New York brokerage firm of Cady, Roberts and Company had learned from a director of Curtiss-Wright that the latter company was about to cut its dividend. The brokerage representative sold short Curtiss-Wright shares – and was held responsible for making use of information originating privately with someone else.)

The editorial reaction from newspapers across the country was immediate and emotional. The *Wall Street Journal* said that the infrequency of such insider charges illustrated the good faith of businessmen generally. It also pointed up the difficulties of enforcing rules that govern the behavior of corporate executives in their stock market dealings:

> An executive, for example, may simply have a general feeling, based partly on past performance but on no tangible certainties, that his company's stock is going to rise; no reason exists in law or ethics why he should be prevented from imparting his information to friends or associates. That's fairly simple, but the problem can get complicated while still on the side of virtue.
>
> By way of illustration, one of the defendants in the SEC case [Executive Vice-president Fogarty] has said his

purchase of that stock in the days just before the announcement of the Ontario discovery were made not on that basis but on the basis of publicly announced – and important – developments in Utah and North Carolina. Whether true or not, the point is that it certainly could be true.

The *Engineering and Mining Journal* recognized the necessity for secrecy following the first indications of a discovery, and judged:

It strikes us that the company acted in its own best interests during the discovery and early evaluation period, but events forced its hand prematurely.

The *Northern Miner*, ignoring the fact that Canada at that time had no laws whatsoever governing the activities of insiders, decided the Securities and Exchange Commission was going altogether too far. "Where will it end?" asked a lead editorial in the *Miner*, part of which stated:

Only one hole was drilled in the period from November through to early April. [In that period, the company expanded its land holdings from next to nothing to something like 75,000 acres, no mean trick, and one that could be of advantage to its shareholders.] One hole does not make a mine – it never has, and it never will – yet the SEC case dwells substantially on this point.

The *Miner* apparently chose to forget that its ace reporter, Graham Ackerley, had described his reaction to the core from K-55-1 as the "thrill of a lifetime."

With the annual meeting only three days away, Texas Gulf hurried into preparation a lengthy statement to be made by President Claude Stephens. Two public relations consultants were flown to Houston to draft the statement, but the final product was mostly the work of the company's lawyers. "As I am sure you are all aware," it began; at the conclusion, Stephens said:

> I am pleased to inform you that your board is satisfied that no element of bad faith or over-reaching was involved in any purchase by officers or directors, or in the granting of the stock options. However, we recognize that others, influenced by hindsight and the magnitude of the Timmins discovery, might have concern. Because of this possibility, each of the officers and directors involved was concerned that his purchases might reflect adversely upon the company and its management. Therefore, each of the individuals has concluded that decisive action should be taken to remove any doubt whatsoever. To this end at a board meeting held on the morning of April 15, 1965, each of the officers and directors who purchased stock offered to turn over to the company all profits accruing to him as a result of purchases between November 1, 1963, a date prior to the commencement of our initial drill hole on Kidd 55, and 10:55 a.m. on April 16, 1964.

The board's resolution said: "This board commends the integrity of these individuals and expresses its gratitude and appreciation for their action."

Stephens further announced that he and Charles Fogarty had offered to yield stock options granted to them three months in advance of the discovery announcement at a price of $23.87 per share.

Said the board, ". . . in recording the voluntary surrender of these options by Messrs. Stephens and Fogarty, the board of directors reiterates its earlier expressions of appreciation and commendation of the integrity and unselfish loyalty of these individuals."

The SEC, however, sniffingly rejected these offers and insisted on pursuing its case.

There were 250 shareholders at the annual meeting of April 22, more than had attended any Texas Gulf annual meeting in memory. None asked about the SEC lawsuit in a question-and-answer period that followed the meeting. Few seemed even concerned. The questions were directed to the results of further explorations at Kidd 55, and as to whether there were any plans to increase dividends.

In Washington that day, a government official was caught in the backwash of the SEC action. Herbert Klotz, the 47-year-old Assistant Secretary of Commerce who had worked for the election of President John F. Kennedy, resigned his $14,700-a-year job following the disclosure that he had bought Texas Gulf shares as a result of a conversation with Ken Darke's girlfriend, Nancy Atkinson. The announcement of Klotz's resignation gave no reason: "Secretary of Commerce John Connor announced today that assistant secretary Herbert W. Klotz has submitted his resignation and that it has been accepted by the President." Klotz himself calculated that he had made a paper profit of $14,600 from the purchase of the options. It was the first case in which an official of the Johnson administration had been accused of improper conduct in a matter involving money. He certainly had become involved innocently enough.

Shareholders at the Texas Gulf annual meeting might have been apathetic towards the SEC complaint, but elsewhere some were preparing to exploit the new opportunities opened to them by the government charges. A day after the annual meeting, two former shareholders sued the company for more than $25 million, charging that Texas Gulf had withheld information about the Kidd discovery and caused them to sell their shares at prices far below their true market value. Dr. Isidore Yasuna, medical director of a New York hospital, sought $25 million in punitive damages and $8,400 in actual damages. Yasuna's suit said he sold 100 shares on March 23, 1964, at $24.50 a share, and 100 more shares on April 16 the same year for $31.50. Yasuna said these prices were "wholly inadequate," and maintained that his stock was worth at least $71.50 per share. Victor M. Cannon, a professor of English from Long Island, said in another suit that he lost $20,569 by selling 500 shares on April 15, the day before the discovery announcement. Cannon said that in selling his shares he had relied on the announcement of April 12, which described rumors of the discovery as "premature and possibly misleading."

That was just the beginning. Within weeks, disgruntled shareholders of numerous corporations were challenging the judgment and the good faith of their corporate managers. Texas Gulf was the main target: Four months after the SEC charges, 120 shareholders and former shareholders had filed at least 16 private suits seeking millions of dollars in damages. The Securities and Exchange Commission had had 400 inquiries from other angry shareholders. In other cases, Yale Express System Inc. of New York was the object of 17 investor suits, most of which charged that the company had failed to give adequate and prompt information about the state of its financial affairs. And Belock Instrument Corporation of New York was charged in a similar court action by a shareholder who contended he had paid inflated prices for his stock because the company's public reports overstated assets and income. The potential for an epidemic of shareholder actions frayed the nerves of the business community.

There was no way to measure the impact of this publicity on the confidence of investors. There was no way to judge how this new atmosphere was affecting the disclosure policies of publicly owned corporations. Once, the Securities and Exchange Commission had bared its sharpest teeth at companies inclined to say too much too soon. Now the relentless pressure from the New York Stock Exchange and other institutions for prompt and full disclosure was complicated by the fear of public misinterpretation of corporate pronouncements.

Texas Gulf Sulphur Company was shortly to begin its formal rebuttal to the SEC *charges.* Top officers of the company demanded a judgment dismissing the complaints against them, and categorically denied any violation of the Securities Exchange Act or regulations of the Securities and Exchange Commission.

> Anyone familiar with the company's total communications could not possibly draw the conclusions that the officers wanted to depress the value of the stocks and to mislead the stockholders and the public about the company's future prospects. . . . The SEC complaint has been an open invitation to suits by former stockholders. These former stockholders have obviously been misled by the distorted picture of the company presented in the complaint and the interpretations of it which have been published. It has been erroneously concluded by some observers that "insiders made a killing." Nothing is further from the truth. We did not.

It was left to the courts to decide this issue in a confrontation that was soon to begin but which still may take many years to resolve.

Also unresolved is the question of who initiated the SEC's action against Texas Gulf. In his column, "Insider's Washington" in the *Houston Chronicle*, on April 26, 1965, Charles Bartlett wrote:

> Officials close to Pres. Johnson suspect that he encouraged the SEC to bring indictments against insiders of the Texas Gulf Sulphur Company as a warning to business-

men. The company failed twice previously to heed private White House admonitions against raising prices. SEC commissioners would have been unlikely to risk the administration's relations with business by making these unprecedented charges unless they had a green light from the president.

Chapter Twenty

TEXAS GULF GOES TO COURT

At the trial of Texas Gulf Sulphur Company and its directors, officers, and employees, the Securities and Exchange Commission attempted to convict the defendants on a scrupulously strict standard of performance. The SEC quoted the late Mr. Justice Anthony Cardozo of the court of appeals of New York:

> Many forms of conduct permissible in a workaday world for those acting at arm's length are forbidden to those bound by fiduciary ties. A trustee is held to something stricter than the morals of the market place. Not honesty alone, but the punctilio of an honor the most sensitive is then the standard of behavior.

Cardozo had said:

A host of impoverished investors stand ready to attest that there are dangers in spreading belief about half truth and untruths, that when such information is given currency in the market, shareholders, the investing public, the financial community, lies at the mercy of the purveyors of such information or misinformation.

The Securities and Exchange Commission used Cardozo's words in expressing its intent to "drag to the light and pillory" the executives of Texas Gulf.

If there was a phrase that summed up the company's defense, it was that "hindsight is a standard no man should be judged by." It was the contention of Texas Gulf that there were numerous other favorable corporate developments at the time of the Kidd Township exploration, all known to the public, which might just as well have been the motivation for the purchase of stock by company personnel.

Judge Dudley J. Bonsal of the United States District Court, southern district of New York, presided at the trial which was certain to have important and lasting consequences for future business morality. The central issue was whether the information gathered from the first drill hole, K-55-1, was "material" – a legal word which defies precise definition. If the assays from the first drill core had been made public in November, 1963, would they have had an impact on the market price of Texas Gulf shares? Would they have affected the judgment of a prudent investor?

There was intense excitement in the business community while they awaited Judge Bonsal's decision. The *New York Times* described the situation at the end of the trial:

New York: Both sides rested last week in the case of the Securities and Exchange Commission versus Texas Gulf Sulphur Co. et al.

After 2,660 pages of transcript, 61 witnesses and 17

days of trial, Judge Dudley B. Bonsal, who has been hearing the case without a jury, scheduled summations for June 21 and set a deadline of July 5 for the filing of post-trial briefs.

No one is willing to predict when Judge Bonsal will hand down his decision, but no matter which side wins an appeal seems certain.

Few issues of fact are involved, but there are some major questions of law. The way in which they are ultimately resolved will have an important bearing on what corporate officers, directors and employees can do in the stock market.

Judge Bonsal decided in favor of Texas Gulf. He said that the test of "material" information must be a conservative one and that "the results of K-55-1 were too 'remote' when considered in light of the size of Texas Gulf, the scope of its activities, and the number of its outstanding shares, to have had any significant impact on the market." This meant dismissal of the suit for Texas Gulf, and for 11 of its 13 officers and employees. In Bonsal's view it did not, however, excuse geophysicist Hugh Clayton, who bought shares the day before the discovery announcement, and Secretary David Crawford, who ordered the purchase of shares at midnight on April 15. Clayton and Crawford, in Bonsal's judgment, were out to "beat the news."

The SEC appealed the dismissal, and two years later, the United States Court of Appeals decided on a different interpretation of the word "material." The court agreed with Bonsal that insiders should be required to abstain from buying their own company's shares only in "those situations which are essentially extraordinary in nature and which are reasonably certain to have a substantial effect on the market price of the security if disclosed." But this didn't mean the test of materiality had to be conservative.

The court unanimously held that a corporate insider in possession of important inside information about his corporation may not trade in the corporation's stock without disclosing that information, even though his transactions are not face-to-face but on a national securities exchange. This duty was unanimously held to apply to employees of the corporation, as well as to its top officers. The court also held unanimously that insiders may not pass such inside information to others for their use in securities transactions; the majority included recommendations on the basis of important inside information within this prohibition.

While Bonsal said the results of K-55-1 were too "remote" to have any significant impact on the stock market, the appeal court said:

> . . . knowledge of the possibility, which surely was more than marginal, of the existence of a mine of the vast magnitude indicated by the remarkably rich drill core . . . might well have affected the price of Texas Gulf stock and would certainly have been an important fact to a reasonable, if speculative, investor in deciding whether he should buy, sell or hold.

The appeal court reversed the dismissal of the charges against Texas Gulf and the other defendants, and in the light of its broader definition of the word "material," sent the case back down to Dudley Bonsal. At this writing, it rests there.

However, Francis G. Coates, the Texas Gulf Director who had purchased 500 shares of stock through his son-in-law 34 minutes before the Dow Jones first announced the discovery, did not await Bonsal's reconsideration. Instead he has now asked the Supreme Court to review the decision of the Court of Appeals, as has Counsel Harold Kline.

A key point in his appeal to the court is that corporate officials simply don't know what the SEC expects of them:

The confusion engendered by the Commission's varying interpretations [of insider trading limitations] is compounded by its refusal, even up to the present, to define the standard of conduct which it claims already exists. . . .

Meanwhile, Texas Gulf was running into serious trouble of an entirely unexpected nature back in Timmins.

Many people in Timmins resent Texas Gulf, for considering the extent of the ore find, surprisingly little benefit has come to the town – in fact a number of people were losers because of it. Practically none of the Timmins residents had purchased Texas Gulf stock and made money; instead, most had bought into the penny disasters like Windfall and Bunker Hill which had sprung up around the Texas Gulf Sulphur discovery, and, of course, those people lost their money.

Thus it was with increasing annoyance that the merchants and union officials saw the rich ore being shovelled out of the ground from its open pit and put into trains to be shipped to the U.S. for smelting. The commonest remark heard in the town was, "Well at least they could refine it here in Timmins and put another 300 men to work." Texas Gulf saw it quite differently, for it was considerably more profitable to refine the ore elsewhere instead of building a new refinery. They saw no reason to change their policy, for local good will seemed relatively irrelevant to them and certainly could not add anything to the dividend cheques.

The company made one other serious error. It is the custom in Ontario for large natural resource companies extracting metal ore from the ground to give substantial cash donations to the governing Conservative party prior to each election campaign. In return, the mining industry has been blessed with low taxes and practically no requirements or standards relative to air and water pollution. Texas Gulf, perhaps because they were new to Ontario customs, did not make the expected contributions to the Conservative war chest.

On March 21, 1969, the matter came to a head. The city council of Timmins voiced the mounting anger at the continued export of ore in a telegram, which they sent to their legislative representative, Bill Ferrier, the young minister who had been elected just a year-and-a-half before from the opposition NDP party. The telegram read as follows:

Re: Processing Facilities of the Texas Gulf Sulphur Company with Respect to the Kidd Creek Mine Development. The people of the Porcupine require your immediate action in their battle for survival.

Within a short time, Texas Gulf Sulphur will announce the building of a Smelter and/or a Refinery. Indications point to a location other than the Porcupine. If our apprehensions are well founded, the life blood of this area will be drained away daily. Ores mined locally will be transported by the Ontario Northland Railway, and at a tremendous profit, to other Provinces and Countries to make work for the people there. This process has already started.

Our local gold mines, because of high operating costs without compensating increase in revenue for gold production, are nearing depletion. Industry other than mining and lumbering find it of no advantage to locate here away from the markets. Employment opportunities are scarce and our young leave for areas of opportunity.

We need a base on which to build a future. Industry will not do it, and it is not expected that it will, if economics do not justify it. This requires political action by Governments.

As leaders of our Community, we have had the opportunity of meeting officials of the Texas Gulf Sulphur

Company on various occasions and our relations with them over the years have been good. We all know, that from the Company's standpoint, the economics of these processing facilities dictate the future location of the same.

We urge the Government of the Province of Ontario to take action which will make it mandatory for Texas Gulf Sulphur Company to build its smelters and/or refinery here in the Timmins Area. The Government has said it insists on processing in Ontario. The Texas Gulf Sulphur Company has announced that it would build its processing facilities in Ontario. What is needed as part of Government's war on regional disparity is to go a step further than having it built in Ontario, and insist on processing at the mine site.

We want to share in this . . . PROVINCE OF OPPORTUNITY . . . to have our region developed and prosper to the same extent as the South. We will not attract industry when the existing industry will not process here, so the Government must act. It is of utmost importance that a Smelter be located in this area to lay the ground work for future Northern development. Governments have recognized, at least of late, the necessity for pouring funds in slow growth and fluctuating growth areas in order to get development on its way. A better way of achieving these worthwhile goals without expenditure of funds is to regulate location of processing facilities. We urge you to take whatever means are required to insure that Texas Gulf Sulphur Company process ores in the general area of the mine. These are Ontario Resources and Government can regulate the exploitation of them so as to achieve the most equitable distribution of wealth and opportunities as is possible.

No better opportunity will ever present itself to Governments for helping non-industrialized Northern Ontario to obtain its rightful share of the riches of this Province.

> Mayor and Council
> Corporation of the Town of Timmins
> Timmins-Porcupine Development
> Commission

That day Ferrier rose in the Ontario legislature to demand the suspension of ordinary business in order to debate the urgency of Texas Gulf Sulphur's building a smelter in Timmins. He insisted that the matter was urgent and demanded that the Minister of Mines take some action.

The Ontario Department of Mines has never been accused of pressing mining companies excessively in matters of the public interest – but here was a chance for the new mines minister to show his independence without feeling repercussions inside the Conservative cabinet. He dispatched the following letter to Richard Mollison at the Texas Gulf Sulphur Company:

Dear Dick:

Over the past year, the frank and co-operative attitude of you and your colleagues in our various meetings has been appreciated by me and by the government.

As a result of our meetings and your studies, under date of April 7th last, you have written to me indicating certain plans and making enquiries of me relating in particular to certain matters respecting hydro rates and transportation costs.

As well, our own progressive development of Resources policy and the continued mounting of public pressure require us, in our view, to make public very shortly a more detailed and definitive statement of standards respecting Mineral Resources development and the targets we expect those in the private sector to reach, so that we may realize our already-announced objectives.

Our purpose, as you know, has not been to embarrass your Company by harsh statements indicating that government policy has been forcing the Company into steps which it was reluctant to take, and partly because of this, details of our methods to encourage processing of our mineral resources in Canada have not even yet been publicly revealed. But we feel, in fairness to all concerned, and especially bearing in mind the position of potential developers and investors, that I should make a detailed statement in the Legislature before too long.

Naturally, if at the same time I could also announce the plans of Texas Gulf Sulphur in relation to at least its proposed zinc smelter, it might also remove any stigma that the Company is and has been developing its plans solely at the urging of the government.

In more detailed reply to your letter of April 7th, and on behalf of the Government the following points should now be made:

1. As is obvious from our recently-introduced statutory changes, we do insist as a matter of irrevocable government policy, that a smelter be built in Canada to process zinc concentrates from the Kidd Creek mine of your subsidiary, Ecstall Mining Ltd.

2. It is the strong desire, even though we feel that we cannot insist upon it, that the zinc smelter should be built in the Timmins area. . . .

4. Finally we feel that the time is over-due for definite action. Assuming that construction could start this calendar year, we would like to hear from you why actual production from the smelter could not be expected by the end of 1971 or at the latest by the middle of 1972. May I have your observations?

With warmest personal regards,

Yours truly,
Allan F. Lawrence,
Minister.

In return the minister promised tax, power, and transportation concessions to the company.

It took Texas Gulf only four days to cave in. On April 25, they announced with great fanfare that the mining smelter was to be built in Timmins at a cost of 50 million dollars. The company could well afford it.

In 1967, sales and earnings of Texas Gulf Sulphur Company were the highest in the company's history by a wide margin. President Claude Stephens said this performance reflected "continuing strong demand for sulphur and the rapid development of our diversification programs into other natural resources." The 1967 annual report said only that the Kidd Creek mine had made "a substantial contribution to the company's increased sales and earnings" during its first full year of operations – probably a fair statement, since earnings increased to $6.15 per share from $2.80 per share the year before.

1968 was the first full year of the operation of the company's huge new mine. Kidd Creek produced ore concentrates containing 13,396,000 ounces of silver. The concentrates held 562,400 tons of 52% zinc, 205,400 of 23% copper, and 96,000 tons of lead. As a result of this output, "Metal income has become a close second to sulphur, the mainstay of our business," the annual report said.

The company reported earnings of $6.99 a share. "Looking ahead, 1969 earnings from metals are expected to improve even further with higher tonnage sales of zinc concentrates."

Texas Gulf clearly is still not prepared to beat the drums over the discovery of the Kidd Creek mine. Despite further drilling of the orebody, the company has not revised its 55-million ton estimate of June, 1964 – an amount which, in any case, makes it more valuable than all the gold mined from the Porcupine area since the beginning of this century.

EPILOGUE

Where will the backlash from the SEC attack end? Perhaps the angriest comment about the Texas Gulf case came from *Barron's,* the financial weekly:

> This is not regulation – it is bureaucracy run wild. For decades, Wall Street and Main Street alike have clung to the delusion that the SEC was designed to protect investors. The Texas Gulf Sulphur case should forever shatter that myth. At each fresh aggrandizement of the agency's power, each assault on personal freedom, brokers and businessmen have beat a retreat under the ignoble standard, "We can live with it." Gentlemen, can you live with the police state?

In Canada exactly the contrary view is held. The TGS discovery followed by the speculation in worthless muskeg has once again pointed up the little protection given to investors in the country. Here the insider laws are weak and full of loopholes, and disclosures to shareholders are not required by law. The TGS case dramatically illustrated the impotence of present legislation and the attitude of the present government.

For at the same time that the SEC was prosecuting TGS directors and employees for their actions an episode in Canada didn't even produce a yawn from the government.

On July 10, 1964, Mr. Eric Scott, a senior partner in a member brokerage house at the Toronto Stock Exchange and a former chairman of the Board of Governors of the Toronto Stock Exchange, sent out the following wire to all the branch offices of his firm.

> To All – re Windfall – While this situation is still very speculative, from what I have been able to find out, I believe your clients should be long some stock . . so that if it is big, and it could be, they will be able to increase their holdings with an average under the market.

Sixteen minutes before he dispatched the wire Mr. Scott purchased 1,000 shares of Windfall for his own account. Five other employees of Scott's firm purchased stock in Windfall prior to the dispatch of the telegram.

Perhaps the U.S. government through the SEC overprotects U.S. investors. No Canadian government has yet reached the point where they feel their investors deserve adequate protection. If you, as a Canadian or American investor, intend to purchase stock in a Canadian corporation, the rule is still, "Let the buyer beware."

INDEX